FREEDOM WARS

WHAT YOU CAN DO TO PRESERVE YOUR RIGHTS

JOHN W. WHITEHEAD

TRI PRESS ®
Charlottesville, Virginia

The Freedom Wars: What You Can Do to Preserve Your Rights

© 2010 Glass Onion Productions

Printed in the United States of America by TRI PRESS®

For information, contact:

TRI PRESS
Post Office Box 7482
Charlottesville, VA 22906-7482

ISBN: 978-0-9772331-8-2

Book design by Chris Combs

Dedicated to my good friend Nat Hentoff,
a true freedom fighter and warrior journalist with a
deep-seated intolerance of injustice.

THE FREEDOM WARS

WHAT PATRIOTS DO

"No matter that patriotism is too often the refuge of scoundrels. Dissent, rebellion, and all-around hell-raising remain the true duty of patriots."
— Barbara Ehrenreich[1]

In early 2010, I was invited to speak to a group of affluent, upper middle class retirees. The host's estate was extensive, his home airy and spacious, original art graced the walls, and the guests ranged from dignitaries to activists from the civil rights era.

I had been invited to lead a discussion on ways to minimize political polarization and find common ground, and I agreed, hoping that these people, who are well-educated, well-connected and well-to-do, would want to get involved in the freedom struggle and effect change within their spheres of influence. Instead, I came face to face with those I've been writing about for years— materially comfortable, disconnected from reality and totally oblivious to what's been going on in the American government as far as the erosion of our civil liberties and the amassing of power by the federal government.

I quickly realized that what these people call polarization is actually Americans challenging the status quo, especially challenging the so-called government elite. To my surprise, I found myself on the receiving end of a group lecture in which I was reprimanded for being too negative in my views of the government. I was also informed that I need to have "faith" in our leaders and refrain from criticizing our president because Americans still live in the best country in the world. In other words, my patriotism was called into question.

But is this really what patriotism or loving your country is all about? If so, then those who founded America, and the great freedom fighters of our own times, would be considered unpatriotic.

I felt like a radical extremist just sitting there. After all, I spend my time calling government leaders to account for their actions, and when they fail to abide by the Constitution, I actively and vocally exercise my rights as a citizen and encourage others to do so as well. In fact, the First Amendment does more than give us a right to criticize our country—*it makes it a civic duty*.

It didn't take long for me to see that my view of what it means to be American was diametrically opposed to that of the group. I belong to the camp that equates patriotism with activism—even when that activism may be perceived as extremism. Martin Luther King Jr. put it best when, after being accused of extremism, he responded, "The question is not whether we will be extremists, but what kind of extremist will you be?"[2]

This group, however, which is representative of a substantial cross-section of Americans, seems to think that you're not a good citizen if you criticize the government, and that faith in the government and a positive attitude are enough to get us through the day. Comfortable in their materialism, they have come to believe that being a good citizen means doing one thing—voting.

The problem we face today, however, is that America requires more than voters. It requires doers—a well-informed and very active group of doers—if we are to have any chance of holding the government accountable and maintaining our freedoms.

After all, it was not idle rhetoric that prompted the Framers of the Constitution to begin with the words "We the people." In the words of former United States Supreme Court Chief Justice Earl Warren, throughout the extraordinary document that is the Constitution and Bill of Rights, "there is an implicit assumption that we, the people, will preserve our democratic rights by acting responsibly in our enjoyment of them."[3]

The Framers of the Constitution knew very well that whenever and wherever democratic governments had failed, it was because the people had abdicated their responsibility as guardians of freedom. The Framers also knew that whenever in history the people denied this responsibility, an authoritarian regime arose which eventually denied the people the right to govern themselves. All governments, it must be remembered, fall into two classifications: those with a democratic form and those that are authoritarian, ruled by an individual or some oligarchic elite.

Thus, the ultimate responsibility for maintaining our freedoms rests with the people. Acting responsibly, however, means that there are certain responsibilities and duties without which our rights would become meaningless. Duties of citizenship extend beyond the act of voting, which is only the first step in acting responsibly. Citizens must be willing to stand and fight to protect their freedoms. At the very least, it will entail criticizing the government. It may even include outright acts of resistance. This is patriotism in action.

Responsible citizenship also means being outraged at the loss of others' freedoms, even when our own are not directly threatened. And it means remembering that the prime function of any free government is to protect our freedoms against those who would abuse them or take them away.

Is it possible to be patriotic and love one's country while disagreeing with the government or going to court to fight for freedom? It is not only possible but vitally necessary to the survival of our republic. Love of country will sometimes entail carrying a picket sign or going to jail, if necessary, to preserve liberty. And it will mean speaking up for those with whom you might disagree. Tolerance for dissent, we must remember, is a vital characteristic of the citizens of a democratic society. As Supreme Court Justice Oliver Wendell Holmes said, "If there is any principle of the Constitution that more imperatively calls for attachment than any other, it is the principle of free thought—not free thought for those who agree with us but freedom for the thought that we hate."[4]

Loving your country does not mean being satisfied with the status quo or the way government is being administered. Government invariably, possibly inevitably, oversteps its authority. As human beings are not perfect, governments, because they are constructs of human beings, will necessarily be imperfect as well.

Love of country, it must be emphasized, is always strengthened by both a knowledge of history and of the Constitution and a willingness to act on that knowledge when and if the need arises. "If we have no appreciation of the past," Justice Warren recognized, "we can have little understanding of the present or vision for the future."[5]

The problems facing our generation are numerous and are becoming incredibly complex. Technology, which has developed at a rapid pace, offers those in power more invasive and awesome possibilities than ever before. Never in American history has there been a more pressing need to maintain the barriers in the Constitution erected by our Founders to check governmental power and abuse.

We're at a very crucial crossroads in American history. We have to be well-informed, not only about current events, but well-versed in the basics of our rights and duties as citizens. If not, in perceived times of crisis, we may very well find ourselves in the clutches of a governmental system that is alien to everything America stands for. And as astute political leaders have recognized, the mass of citizens will continue to be misinformed and easily led. Therein is the menace to our freedoms.

As Hermann Goering, one of Adolf Hitler's top military leaders, opined:

> It is always a simple matter to drag the people along, whether it is a democracy, or a fascist dictatorship, or a parliament, or a communist dictatorship. Voice or no voice, the people can always be brought to the bidding of the leaders. That is easy. All you have to do is to tell them they are being attacked, and denounce the pacifists for lack of patriotism and exposing the country to danger. It works the same in any country.[6]

PART ONE

"As nightfall does not come all at once, neither does oppression. In both instances, there is a twilight when everything remains seemingly unchanged. And it is in such twilight that we all must be most aware of change in the air—however slight—lest we become unwitting victims of the darkness."
>   —William O. Douglas,
>   U.S. Supreme Court Justice

CHAPTER ONE
WHAT IT MEANS TO BE AN AMERICAN

> *"The fate of the country does not depend on how you vote at the polls—the worst man is as strong as the best at that game; it does not depend on what kind of paper you drop into the ballot-box once a year, but on what kind of man you drop from your [bed] chamber into the street every morning..."*
>
> —Henry David Thoreau[1]

Following 9/11, it became increasingly clear that something had changed about America. Not only was this change evident in how governmental agencies had come to view us as citizens, but a more troubling change was the way the American people came to view themselves. Suddenly, Americans had ceased to be the people they once were.

Once a citizenry that generally fomented a rebellion, founded a country, and wrote the Declaration of Independence, the Constitution and the Bill of Rights, most Americans today have become more or less compliant lambs, beguiled by materialism and technology and woefully ignorant of the rights found in their great freedom documents. And if the threat of a terrorist attack (no matter how tenuous) is raised, most are willing to give over their rights if it makes them *feel* safer. In fact, the majority of Americans don't believe the government has gone far enough in protecting the country from terrorism. Nor do they believe the government's anti-terror policies have gone too far in restricting their civil liberties.[2]

Thus, the most pressing issue today is not terrorism. Nor is it healthcare or the economy. Rather, the most pressing issue of our day is freedom—or, to be more precise, the loss of freedom internally, domestically and individually. And, unfortunately, more and more Americans are becoming accustomed to, indeed conditioned to, the loss of their rights.

Indeed, much like animals in a zoo, many Americans have come to believe that the zookeeper is friendly. Thus, the greatest threat to our freedoms is not lurking outside our borders in the guise of foreign terrorists or some country purportedly in an "axis of evil." The real menace comes from within. The enemy is *us*—our government of wolves and we the sheep. And there is a lesson here. "Rome did not fall because her armies weakened," writes author Salman Rushdie, "but because Romans forgot what being a Roman meant."[3] Thus, if America collapses into an authoritarian state, it will largely be because many Americans have forgotten what it means to be *American*.

Since our country's inception, America has been synonymous with the concept that there are certain individual rights and freedoms that no one, not even government agents in times of turmoil and change, can violate. This concept is cogently set forth in America's founding document—the Declaration of Independence. The foundational idea that individuals have, in the words of Thomas Jefferson, an inherent right to "Life, Liberty and the pursuit of Happiness" served as the springboard for the Bill of Rights as they were appended to the Constitution. If not for the freedoms enshrined in the first ten amendments to the Constitution—including the freedoms of speech, press, religion and association, the right to assemble and petition the government for a redress of grievances, the right of one accused of a crime to a public jury trial, the right to an attorney and to be confronted by one's accusers, as well as the essential freedom from unreasonable search and seizure—the Constitution would indeed be a rather sterile document.

After Jefferson penned the Declaration, he remarked that he was merely reflecting the American mind. And what was the American mind during the revolutionary era? Early Americans believed there were absolute rights so precious that no government can violate them. As Jefferson declares in the Declaration of Independence: "We hold these truths to be self-evident: that all men are created equal, that they are endowed by their Creator with certain unalienable Rights, that among these are Life, Liberty, and the pursuit of Happiness." What revolutionary thinking! And yet the early American colonists believed these particular principles were not only worth fighting for, they were worth dying for.

What are these "self-evident," or universal, truths? The basic principle is that the people are the masters, not the government, and all people must be treated equally before the law. No one, as Jefferson was later to say, is inferior to another. Shortly before his death in 1826, in the last letter he wrote, Jefferson said: "The mass of mankind has not been born with saddles on their backs, nor a favored few booted and spurred, ready to ride them legitimately, by the grace of God."[4]

Moreover, in order for a governmental power to be legitimate, it has to be conferred by the consent of the people. All men, even presidents, are thus under the rule of law. As the Declaration states: "That to secure these rights, Governments are instituted among Men, deriving their just powers from the consent of the governed." The *presumption* is that such consent is enlightened. And logically, consent has two aspects: consent in establishing government and a continuing consent in operating government.

Finally, the right to change or do away with a government that attempts to undermine these rights rests with the people. As the Declaration's statement of principles concludes, "whenever any form of Government becomes destructive of these ends, it is the Right of the People to alter or abolish it, and to institute new Government, laying its foundation on such principles and organizing its powers in such form, as to them shall seem most likely to effect their Safety and Happiness." The right to resist governmental encroachment, even the right to revolution, therefore, follows logically from these principles.

Jefferson and those who followed his philosophy took it as a rule of thumb that political progress stems from dissent. Under the First Amendment, the people have a right to dissent and to participate in civil disobedience if necessary. Activists such as Martin Luther King, Jr., who forged the civil rights of African-Americans, put Jefferson's revolutionary thinking into action nearly 200 years later. King understood that in order to protect our rights, the people have a right to dissent and, if necessary, to participate in civil disobedience.

Nevertheless, Jefferson knew very well that there are times when even dissent is not enough. Governments are brought into being to protect our inherent rights. When they systematically violate such liberties, however, the people have a right—nay, a duty—to revolt. This was the true spirit of 1776 that moved the American colonists to rebel against a government that was violating their rights. This willingness to stand and fight was what it meant to be an American in the nation's early years.

That said, Jefferson also understood that people were inclined to adopt a so-called zookeeper mentality. As Jefferson writes in the Declaration of Independence, "all experience hath shown that mankind are more disposed to suffer, while evils are sufferable, than to right themselves by abolishing the forms to which they are accustomed."

And suffer the evils we have, especially since 9/11. While most of us were busy attending to the daily routines of life, the government was transformed in such a way as to concentrate power in the executive branch and undermine our system of checks and balances and, thus, the rule of law.

What began with the passage of the USA Patriot Act in the fall of 2001 has snowballed into a massive assault on our constitutional freedoms, our system of government and our fundamental philosophies and way of life. Enabled by a paper tiger Congress, the federal government has repeatedly laid claim to a host of powers, among them the ability to use the military as a police force and spy on Americans while erecting a surveillance state.

Many Americans, however, are unaware that the basic foundations of freedom are being systematically undermined. "The United States today is like a cruise ship on the Niagara River upstream of the most spectacular falls in North America," writes historian and bestselling author Chalmers Johnson. "A few people on board have begun to pick up a slight hiss in the background, to observe a faint haze of mist in the air or on their glasses, to note that the river current seems to be running slightly faster. But no one yet seems to have realized that it is almost too late to head for shore."[5]

CHAPTER TWO
THE STATE OF THE NATION

*"As I look at America today, I am not
afraid to say that I am afraid."*
—Bertram Gross[1]

Ominous developments in America have been a long time coming. Unfortunately, they have, in part, been precipitated by "we the people"—a somnambulant citizenry that has been asleep at the wheel for too long. And while there have been wake-up calls, we have failed to heed the warnings.

Just consider the state of our nation:

We're encased in an electronic concentration camp. The government continues to amass data files on more and more Americans. Everywhere we go, we are watched: at the bank, at the grocery store, at the mall, crossing the street. This loss of privacy is symptomatic of the growing surveillance being carried out on average, law-abiding Americans. Such surveillance gradually poisons the soul of a nation, transforming us from one in which we're presumed innocent until proven guilty to one in which everyone is a suspect and presumed guilty. Thus, the question that must be asked is: can freedom in the United States flourish in an age when the physical movements, individual purchases, conversations and meetings of every citizen are under constant surveillance by private corporations which are interlocked and cooperate with government agencies?

We are metamorphosing into a police state. Governmental tentacles now invade virtually every facet of our lives, with agents of the government listening in on our telephone calls and reading our emails. Technology, which develops at an increasingly rapid pace, offers those in power more invasive and more awesome tools than ever before. Fusion centers—data-collecting agencies spread throughout America, aided by the highly secretive National Security Agency—constantly monitor our communications, everything from our internet activity and web searches to text messages, phone calls and emails. This data is then fed to government agencies, which are now interconnected—the CIA to the FBI, the FBI to local police—a relationship which will make a transition to martial law that much easier. We may very well be one terrorist attack away from seeing armed forces on our streets—and the American people may not put up much resistance.

We are plagued by a faltering economy and a monstrous financial deficit that threatens to bankrupt the country. Our national debt is more than $13 trillion (which translates to more than $110,000 per taxpayer), and is expected to nearly double to $20 trillion by 2015. The unemployment rate is over 10% and growing, with millions of Americans out of work and many more forced to subsist on low-paying or part-time jobs. The number of Americans losing their homes has reached catastrophic levels. The number of people receiving food stamps has reached an all-time high, with assistance being doled out to more than 40 million Americans. This translates to one in eight Americans and one out of every four children. The number of children living in poverty is on the rise (18% in 2007). As history illustrates, authoritarian regimes assume more and more power in troubled financial times.

Our representatives in the White House and Congress bear little resemblance to those they have been elected to represent. Many of our politicians live like kings. Chauffeured around in limousines, flying in private jets and eating gourmet meals, all paid for by the American taxpayer, they are far removed from those they represent. What's more, they continue to spend money we don't have on pork-laden stimulus packages while running up a huge deficit and leaving the American taxpayers to foot the bill. And while our representatives may engage in a show of partisan bickering, the Washington elite—that is, the President and Congress—moves forward with whatever it wants, paying little heed to the will of the people.

We are embroiled in global wars against enemies that seem to attack from nowhere. American armed forces are pushed to their limit, spread around the globe and under constant fire. The amount of money spent on the wars in Afghanistan and Iraq is over $1 trillion and is estimated to total somewhere in the vicinity of $3 trillion before it's all over. That does not take into account the ravaged countries that the American military occupies, the thousands of innocent civilians killed (including women and children), or the thousands of American soldiers who have been killed or permanently injured. Nor does it take into account the families of the 1.8 million Americans who have served or are currently serving tours of duty in Iraq and Afghanistan, or the rising numbers of military personnel who have committed or attempted to commit suicide at a rate exceeding that of the national standard. (By late November 2009, more U.S. military lives had been lost to suicide than were killed in the Afghan war.) If you take into account injuries such as hearing loss and diseases including mental illness, the number of American casualties tops more than 500,000.

America's place in the world is also undergoing a drastic shift, with Communist China slated to emerge as the top global economy. Given the extent to which the United States government is financially beholden to China, an authoritarian regime with a powerful military, their influence over how the American government carries out its affairs, as well as how it deals with its citizens, cannot be discounted. As of July 2009, China owned $800.5 billion of American debt—that's 45% of our total (foreign) debt—making them the largest foreign holder of U.S. foreign debt. Little wonder, then, that the U.S. government has kowtowed to China, hesitant to overtly challenge them on critical issues such as human rights.

As national borders dissolve in the face of spreading globalization, the likelihood increases that our Constitution, which is the supreme law of America, will be subverted in favor of international laws. Efforts have been underway for years to form a North American Union—a fusion of Canada, the United States and Mexico.[2] What that means is that our Constitution will come increasingly under attack.

The corporate media, which all too often acts as a mouthpiece for governmental propaganda, no longer serves a primary function as watchdogs, guarding against encroachments of our rights. Instead, much of the mainstream media has given itself over to mindless, celebrity-driven news, which bodes ill for the country. It doesn't matter whether you're talking about tabloid news, entertainment news or legitimate news shows, there's very little difference between them anymore. Unfortunately, most Americans have bought into the notion that whatever the media happens to report is important and relevant. In the process, Americans are misinformed and have largely lost the ability to ask questions and think analytically. Indeed, most citizens have little, if any, knowledge about their rights or how their government even works.

Finally, I have never seen a country more spiritually beaten down than the United States. We have lost our moral compass. A growing number of our young people now see no meaning or purpose in life.[3] And we no longer have a sense of right and wrong or a way to hold the government accountable. We have forgotten that the essential premise of the American governmental scheme, as set forth in the Declaration of Independence, is that if the government will not be accountable to the people, then it must certainly be accountable to the "Creator."

But what if the government is not accountable to the people or the Creator?

As Thomas Jefferson writes in the Declaration, it is then the right of "the People to alter or abolish it" and form a new government.

CHAPTER THREE

HOW LUCKY IT IS FOR OUR POLITICIANS THAT AMERICANS DO NOT THINK

> *"A nation of sheep will beget a government of wolves."*
> —Edward R. Murrow[1]

"How lucky it is for rulers," Adolf Hitler once said, "that men cannot think."[2] The horrors that followed in Nazi Germany might have been easier to explain if Hitler had been right. But the problem is not so much that people *cannot* think but that they *do not* think. Or if they do think, as in the case of the German people, that thinking becomes muddled and they are, thus, easily led.

Hitler's meteoric rise to power, with the support of the German people, is a case in point. On January 30, 1933, Hitler was appointed chancellor of Germany in full accordance with the country's legal and constitutional principles. When President Paul von Hindenburg died the following year, Hitler assumed the office of president, as well as that of chancellor, but he preferred to use the title Der Fülıer (the leader) to describe himself. This new move was approved in a general election in which Hitler garnered 88 percent of the votes cast.

It cannot be said that the German people were ignorant of Hitler's agenda or his Nazi ideology. Nazi literature, including statements of the Nazi plans for the future, had papered the country for a decade before Hitler came to power. In fact, Hitler's book *Mein Kampf*, which was his blueprint for totalitarianism, sold more than 200,000 copies between 1925 and 1932.

Clearly, the problem was not that the German people did not think but that their thinking was poisoned by the enveloping climate of ideas that they came to accept as important. At a certain point, the trivial became important, and obedience to the government in pursuit of security over freedom became predominant.

We see this same scenario being played out in America today where analytical thinking has given way to a steady diet of mindless entertainment and endless distractions. Rejecting community in favor of self-gratification and isolation, we have in essence become an atomistic society, a characteristic of an emerging totalitarian society.

Connected to all our technological gadgets, we are increasingly disconnected from each other. Even when physically crowded together at entertainment spectacles such as concerts and sports events, we fail to truly communicate with one another. As author Alex Marshall has observed, Americans live "in one of the loneliest societies on the earth."[3] All the while, with little outcry from the citizenry, the government has erected a surveillance state, slowly transforming itself into a centralized, authoritarian bureaucracy that is gobbling up our civil liberties on a daily basis.

Woefully ignorant of the freedoms given us by our forefathers and their subsequent erosion by our government of wolves, Americans rarely come together to strategize on how to maintain their freedoms. Indeed, most Americans do not even engage in meaningful discourse about pressing issues of national and international significance. And as studies show, Americans know much more about trivia (such as the names of the Simpsons and the Three Stooges) than they do the Bill of Rights.[4] For example, less than one percent of adults can name the five rights found in the First Amendment. However, as those who wrote the Constitution warned, a citizenry ignorant of their rights would lose them.

Plain and simple, American educational institutions no longer teach children about their freedoms and how to exercise them. But it gets worse. America currently spends well in excess of $40 billion annually on public education. Yet the numbers are undeniable: in comparing the literacy level of adults in seventeen industrialized countries, America was number ten on the list.[5] And 16- to 25-year-olds underperform their foreign counterparts as well. Moreover, they do so to a greater degree than do Americans over 40. And with the loss of literacy goes a critical ingredient in maintaining freedom—citizens who think analytically.

Thus, ignorant of the very basis of citizenship and overwhelmed by the informational glut of modernity, it is little wonder that many, ostrich-like, are allowing an out-of-control government to move forward unimpeded. Yet while most may feel snug and secure in their technological wombs, they are only temporarily keeping the wolf at bay. Hiding from reality is not the solution. In fact, non-participation by the citizenry only makes matters worse. "Bad officials are elected by good citizens who do not vote," the drama critic George Jean Nathan once remarked.[6] I would add that bad officials will run roughshod over citizens who are clueless.

Thus, for whom does the bell toll? It tolls for us. Everything America was founded upon is in some way being challenged. At stake is the very foundation of the American democratic system. And while it may be easy to fault a particular politician, event or the media— television, in particular—for the state of our nation, the blame, as the renowned CBS newscaster Edward R. Murrow once noted, rests with us—"we the people."

Amid the Red Scare of the 1950s and the Joseph McCarthy era, people were often afraid to speak out against the paranoia being propagated through the media and the government. Fear and paranoia had come to grip much of the American population, and there was a horrible chill in the air. But with great courage, Murrow spoke up. On March 9, 1954, on his CBS television show *See It Now*, Murrow said the following—a statement very apropos for today:

We cannot defend freedom abroad by deserting it at home. The actions of the junior senator from Wisconsin have caused alarm and dismay amongst our allies abroad and given considerable comfort to our enemies, and whose fault is that? Not really his. He didn't create the situation of fear; he merely exploited it, and rather successfully. Cassius was right: "The fault, dear Brutus, is not in our stars but in ourselves."[7]

CHAPTER FOUR

ARE YOU AN ENEMY OF THE STATE?

> *"First they came for the Socialists, and I did not speak out because I was not a Socialist. Then they came for the Trade Unionists, and I did not speak out because I was not a Trade Unionist. Then they came for the Jews, and I did not speak out because I was not a Jew. Then they came for me, and there was no one left to speak for me."*
> —Martin Niemöller,
> Inscription at the
> U.S. Holocaust Museum

The groundwork has been laid for a new kind of government where virtually everyone is a suspect and it will no longer matter if you're innocent or guilty, whether you're a threat to the nation or even if you're a citizen. What will matter is what the president—or whoever happens to be occupying the Oval Office at the time—thinks.

In 2009, the Department of Homeland Security (DHS) issued two reports on right-wing and left-wing extremism. For example, in "Rightwing Extremism: Current Economic and Political Climate Fueling Resurgence in Radicalization and Recruitment," an extremist is defined as anyone who subscribes to a particular political viewpoint. Right-wing extremists, thus, are broadly defined in the report as individuals and groups "that are mainly antigovernment, rejecting federal authority in favor of state or local authority, or rejecting government authority entirely."[1]

This report is problematic on many levels, but several things in particular stand out. First, the report is short on facts and long on generalizations. The DHS states that it has "no specific information that domestic rightwing terrorists are currently planning acts of violence." Nevertheless, it goes on to list a number of scenarios that *could* arise as a result of so-called right-wing extremists playing on the public's fears and discontent over various issues, including the economic downturn, real estate foreclosures and unemployment—all problems created by the government.

Second, the report uses the words terrorist and extremist interchangeably. In other words, voicing what the government would consider to be extremist viewpoints, whether or not you hold left-wing or right-wing political views, is tantamount to being a terrorist. However, if you buy into the government's definition, I could very well be considered a terrorist. So too could John Lennon, Martin Luther King Jr., Roger Baldwin (founder of the ACLU), Patrick Henry, Thomas Jefferson and Samuel Adams—all of these men protested and passionately spoke out against government practices with which they disagreed and would be prime targets under this document. The message to the American people is clear: be careful what you say because if you say something the government doesn't like, you'll become a political enemy.

Third, the 10-page document takes pains to describe the political views of those who would qualify as being a right-wing extremist. For example, you are labeled a right-wing extremist if you exercise your First Amendment rights and voice concerns about a myriad of issues including: policy changes under President Obama; the economic downturn and home foreclosures; the loss of U.S. jobs in manufacturing and construction sectors; and social issues such as abortion, interracial crimes, immigration and same-sex marriage.

DHS also issues a red-flag warning against anyone who promotes "conspiracy theories involving declarations of martial law, impending civil strife or racial conflict, suspension of the U.S. Constitution, and the creation of citizen detention camps."

As a constitutional attorney, I've written on all of these topics at one time or another, and there is nothing conspiratorial about the threats they pose to our rights. Yet according to this document, I am an enemy of the state.

If anyone seems to have a conspiratorial bent, it's the DHS under the Obama administration. Lacking any concrete facts, this document reeks of paranoia on the part of government officials about a possible populist uprising. The danger, however, is that the government has incredible resources to follow through on its fears—which means surveillance and intimidation of citizens who disagree with the government.

The DHS missive on rightwing extremism is even more ominous, especially in light of a U.S. Army War College report issued in the fall of 2008 that called on the military to be prepared for a "violent, strategic dislocation inside the United States."[2] According to the report, such an uprising could be provoked by "unforeseen economic collapse," "purposeful domestic resistance," "pervasive public health emergencies" or "loss of functioning political and legal order"—all related to dissent and protests over America's economic disarray.[3]

This is nothing less than the shot across the bow, a warning that the government will be targeting for surveillance those who disagree with the Obama administration politically. They're going to monitor internet activity and phone calls, as well as what commentators and bloggers have to say. DHS will also be working with state and local government agents (including the police) to conduct surveillance. As the report states: "DHS will be working with its state and local partners over the next several months to ascertain with greater regional specificity the rise in rightwing extremist activity in the United States, with a particular emphasis on the political, economic, and social factors that drive rightwing extremist radicalization." In other words, DHS has nationalized its paranoia.

In taking such an overt stance against political rivals, the government is taking aim at a protected First Amendment right: the right to political speech and thought. Targeting people because of their political views is Nixonesque, a repeat of past tactics to preempt political opposition.

Americans have a right to be disgruntled. They shouldn't be censored, subjected to surveillance or intimidated into silence simply because they take to the streets, protest or choose to carry a picket sign that attacks government policies.

Why should any American be treated like an enemy of the state just because we choose to exercise our constitutional rights?

CHAPTER FIVE

BIG BROTHER WANTS
TO KNOW ALL ABOUT YOU

"This is Big Brother at its worst."
—Congressman Ted Poe (R-TX)[1]

Over the years, I have been barraged with phone calls, letters and emails from Americans expressing their dismay over the American Community Survey, an invasive "census" form that randomly hits select households on a continuous basis. Unlike the traditional census, which collects data every ten years, the American Community Survey is taken every year at a cost of hundreds of millions of dollars. And at 28 pages (with an additional 16-page instruction packet), it contains some of the most detailed and intrusive questions ever put forth in a census questionnaire. These concern matters that the government simply has no business knowing, including a person's job, income, physical and emotional health, family status, place of residence and intimate personal and private habits.

As one frustrated survey recipient, Beth, shared with me in an email:

When we first read through the American Community Survey, we thought it was an ID theft scam. I showed it to a lawyer friend of mine. She had never heard of the survey and warned it could be a scam. She said if she'd received this, she would call her congressman and senator to find out if scams such as this were happening to warn others. So I called Washington DC. They in turn told me to call our senator's office in my state—which I did. I was referred to the Justice Department, who then referred me to my county representative. When I called my county representative, my call was shifted to a Census Bureau employee placed in their offices to field questions about the survey. The Census Bureau representative told me the survey was not a scam. She could not tell me whether or not to fill it out, but said if we chose not to, there could be hefty fines and jail time associated with not doing so. She was no help at all and was evasive in answering my questions.

As Beth found out, the survey is not voluntary. Answering the questions is not a polite request from the U.S. Census Bureau. You are legally obligated to answer. If you refuse, the fines are staggering. For every question not answered, there is a $100 fine. And for every intentionally false response to a question, the fine is $500. Therefore, if a person representing a two-person household refused to fill out *any* questions or simply answered nonsensically, the total fines could range from upwards of $10,000 and $50,000 for noncompliance.

While the penalties for not answering are outrageous,

the questions are both ludicrous and insulting. For example, the survey asks how many persons live in your home, along with their names and detailed information about them such as their relationship to you, marital status, race, physical, mental and emotional problems, and so on. The survey also asks how many bedrooms and bathrooms you have in your house, along with the kind of fuel used to heat your home, the cost of electricity, what type of mortgage you have, the amount of your monthly mortgage payments, property taxes and so on. This questionnaire also requires you to detail how many days you were sick last year, how many automobiles you own, whether you have trouble getting up the stairs and, amazingly, what time you leave for work every morning and how long it takes you to get there. When faced with the prospect that government agents could covertly enter your home and rifle through your personal belongings, do you really want the government knowing exactly when you're away from home?

As if the survey's asinine questions and highly detailed inquiries into your financial affairs weren't bad enough, you're also expected to violate the privacy of others by supplying the names and addresses of your friends, relatives and employer. And the questionnaire stipulates that you provide such information on the people in your home as their educational levels, how many years of schooling they completed, what languages they speak and when they last worked at a job, among other things.

Americans being ordered by the government to inform and spy on their family and friends? It's not too far off from the scenario George Orwell envisioned in his futuristic novel *Nineteen Eighty-Four*. "The family," writes Orwell, "had become in effect an extension of the Thought Police. It was a device by means of which everyone could be surrounded night and day by informers who knew him intimately."[2]

Granted, some of the questions in the American Community Survey may appear fairly routine. However, the danger rests in not knowing exactly *how* the government plans to use this vast amount of highly personal information. For instance, if the financial information you provide on the survey does not coincide with your tax returns, whether such a discrepancy was intentional or not, you could be targeted for an IRS audit.

Another concern with this intrusive questionnaire is that it signifies yet another step toward the establishment of a permanent surveillance state. Everywhere we look these days, we are either being watched, taxed or some bureaucrat is placing another bit of information in our government files. And with the American Community Survey, the federal bureaucracy is thrusting its expansive tentacles toward us in an attempt to invade every aspect of our lives.

This is not what the Founders intended. As Article I of the U.S. Constitution makes clear, the census is to be taken every ten years for the sole purpose of congressional redistricting.

The Founders envisioned a simple head count of the number of people living in a given area so that numerically equal congressional districts could be maintained. There is no way that the Founders would have authorized the federal government to continuously demand, under penalty of law, such detailed information from the American people.

However, the Founders did not anticipate the massive and meddlesome federal bureaucracy we have today or the daily onslaught of media images and governmental scare tactics designed to keep the modern American distracted and submissive. Sadly, most Americans do not seem to care that their freedoms are being whittled away or else they see no point in resistance. Either way, the reaction is the same: they submit to virtually every government demand, including the highly intrusive and patently unconstitutional American Community Survey.

Thankfully, there are still some Americans out there who value freedom and recognize that it is time to stand up and fight back using whatever peaceful, nonviolent means are available to them. As Beth concludes in her email to me:

> As an American loyal to my country, we have no choice but to stand against this unethical intrusion into our lives. I have called and written to many people. No response. No one seems to be listening. No one seems to care. I intend to vote for those who do care.

CHAPTER SIX

WELCOME TO THE
NEW TOTAL SECURITY STATE

> *"You had to live—did live, from habit that
> became instinct—in the assumption that
> every sound you made was overheard,
> and, except in darkness, every movement
> scrutinized."*
> —George Orwell[1]

The U.S. government now has at its disposal a
technological arsenal so sophisticated and invasive as to
render any constitutional protections null and void. And
these technologies are being used by the government to
invade the privacy of the American people.

Several years ago, government officials acknowledged
that the nefarious intelligence gathering entity known as
the National Security Agency (NSA) had exceeded its legal
authority by eavesdropping on Americans' private email
messages and phone calls. However, these reports barely
scratch the surface of what we are coming to recognize as a
"security/industrial complex"—a marriage of government,
military and corporate interests aimed at keeping average
Americans under constant surveillance.

The increasingly complex security needs of the
massive federal government, especially in the areas of

defense, surveillance and data management, have been met within the corporate sector, which has shown itself to be a powerful ally that both depends on and feeds the growth of governmental bureaucracy. For example, in the wake of the 9/11 terrorist attacks, the corporate homeland security business is booming to such an extent that it has eclipsed mature enterprises like movie-making and the music industry in annual revenue. Government spending on security provided by private corporations now exceeds $1 trillion.

Money, power, control. There is no shortage of motives fueling the convergence of mega-corporations and government. But who will pay the price? The American people, of course, and you can be sure that it will take a toll on more than our pocketbooks. "You have government on a holy mission to ramp up information gathering and you have an information technology industry desperate for new markets," says Peter Swire, the nation's first privacy counselor in the Clinton administration. "Once this is done, you will have unprecedented snooping abilities. What will happen to our private lives if we're under constant surveillance?"[2]

We're at that point now. Americans have been conditioned to accept routine incursions on their privacy rights. However, at one time, the idea of a total surveillance state tracking one's every move would have been abhorrent to most Americans. That all changed with the 9/11 attacks.

As professor Jeffrey Rosen observes, "Before Sept. 11, the idea that Americans would voluntarily agree to live their lives under the gaze of a network of biometric surveillance cameras, peering at them in government buildings, shopping malls, subways and stadiums, would have seemed unthinkable, a dystopian fantasy of a society that had surrendered privacy and anonymity."[3]

We have, so to speak, gone from being a nation where privacy is king to one where nothing is safe from the prying eyes of government. In search of terrorists hiding among us—the proverbial "needle in a haystack," as one official has termed it—the government has taken to monitoring all aspects of our lives, from cell phone calls and emails to internet activity and credit card transactions. Much of this data is being fed through fusion centers—state and regional intelligence centers across the country that collect data on the average American.

Wherever you go and whatever you do, you are now being watched—especially if you leave behind an electronic footprint. When you use your cell phone, you leave a record of when the call was placed, who you called, how long it lasted and even where you were at the time. When you use your ATM card, you leave a record of where and when you used the card. There is even a video camera at most locations. When you drive a car enabled with GPS, you can be tracked by satellite. And all of this once-private information about your consumer habits, your whereabouts and your activities is now being fed to the U.S. government. The government has nearly inexhaustible resources when it comes to tracking the average citizen's movements, from full-body scanners in airports, electronic wiretapping devices, traffic cameras and biometrics to radio-frequency identification cards, satellites and internet surveillance. Speech recognition technology now makes it possible for the government to carry out massive eavesdropping by way of sophisticated computer systems. Phone calls can be monitored, the audio converted to text files and stored in computer databases indefinitely, and if any "threatening" words are detected—no matter how inane or silly—the record can and most likely will be flagged and assigned to a government agent for further investigation. Added to this, in recent years, federal and state governments, as well as private corporations, have been amassing technological tools aimed at allowing them to monitor internet content. Users are profiled and tracked in order to identify, target and even prosecute them.

In such a climate, everyone is a suspect. And you're guilty until you can prove yourself innocent. To underscore this shift in how the government now views its citizens, just before leaving office, President George W. Bush granted the FBI wide-ranging authority to investigate individuals or groups, regardless of whether they are suspected of criminal activity.

Here's what a lot of people fail to understand, however:

it's not just what you say or do that is being monitored, but how you *think* that is being tracked and targeted. We've already seen this play out on the state and federal level with hate crime legislation that cracks down on hateful thoughts and expression in order to discourage so-called hateful behavior.

Total internet surveillance is merely the next logical step in the government's attempts to predict and, more importantly, control the populace—and it's not as far-fetched as you might think. For example, the powerful National Security Agency (NSA) operates an artificial intelligence system that is designed to anticipate your every move. In a nutshell, the NSA feeds vast amounts of the information it collects to a computer system known as Aquaint (the acronym stands for **A**dvanced **QU**estion **A**nswering for **INT**elligence), which the computer then uses to detect patterns and predict behavior. No information is sacred or spared. Everything from cell phone recordings and logs, emails, text messages, and personal information posted on social networking sites to credit card statements, library circulation records, and credit card histories, etc., is collected by the NSA. One NSA researcher actually quit the program "citing concerns over the dangers in placing such a powerful weapon in the hands of a top-secret agency with little accountability."[4]

So where does this leave us? If we've already been under surveillance for years, largely without our knowledge, what does it matter anyway? And can anything really be done to avoid moving into a total surveillance state? Frankly, technology has developed to such a point that it has outstripped the ability of human beings to control it. It has become virtually autonomous. And in the hands of the surveillance state, technology is largely working against us now.

CHAPTER SEVEN

SCANNERS: NO PLACE TO HIDE

"The only person who is still a private individual in Germany is somebody who is asleep."

—Robert Ley, a member of the Nazi hierarchy[1]

As the surveillance state expands around us, entangling us in a web from which there is no escape, what we used to call "privacy" is fast becoming a thing of the past. In fact, the very latest governmental assaults on our privacy rights take the form of two portable high-tech scanners that are little more than thinly disguised data collection systems aimed at turning unsuspecting Americans into permanent suspects.

The first device, a license-plate recognition scanner that can sweep a parking lot full of cars in under a minute, uses infrared cameras mounted on police cars to constantly scan nearby license plates and check them against police databases. "Police like the devices for their speed and efficiency but mostly for their ability to record thousands of plates and their locations each day," writes journalist Christine Vendel. "The information is loaded wirelessly into a police database and archived for possible searches later."[2] With such a tool at its disposal, the government can retroactively pinpoint exactly where you were on any given day. And if you had the bad luck to be in the wrong place at the wrong time, the burden of proving your innocence will rest with you.

The second device, a mobile version of an airport full-body scanner, will soon be roaming America's streets and neighborhoods.[3] Mounted in nondescript delivery vehicles that enable police or other government agents to blend into urban and other landscapes, these roving x-ray scanners "bounce a narrow stream of x-rays off and through nearby objects, and read which ones come back," thereby producing instantaneous photo-like images of whatever the van passes—whether it be cars, trucks, containers, homes or people. In other words, the government can now do drive-by strip searches of your person and your home, including monitoring what you are doing in the privacy of your home. Even though you may be innocent of any wrongdoing whatsoever, *every* aspect of your life, as well as *every* room of your house and *everything* you do in your house will be under scrutiny by government agents—and can and will be recorded and used against you at a later date.

Together, these surveillance tools form a toxic cocktail for which there is no cure. By subjecting Americans to full-body scans and license-plate readers without their knowledge or compliance and then storing the scans for later use, the government—in cahoots with the corporate state—has erected the ultimate suspect society. In such an environment, there is no such thing as "innocent until proven guilty." We are all potentially guilty of some wrongdoing or other.

Moreover, while these mobile scanners are being sold to the American public as necessary security and safety measures, we can ill afford to forget that such systems are rife with the potential for abuse, not only by government bureaucrats but by the technicians employed to operate them. Just consider the abuses we've already been forced to endure in the wake of the bumbling underwear bomber's December 2009 attempt to blow up a Northwest Airlines flight. In the months that followed, the government's knee-jerk embrace of full-body scanners as a miracle fix rapidly evolved into a headlong and expensive rush to implement scanners in all airports—a program with few guarantees of success and numerous pitfalls, not the least of which is the harrowing toll it is taking on our civil liberties and the risks it poses to our health.

Using either x-ray radiation or radio waves, full-body scanners can "see" through clothing to produce images of an individual's unclothed body, although they are unable to reveal material concealed in body cavities. Critics have likened the scans to "virtual strip searches" because of the degree to which details of the body are revealed. Female travelers have complained about airport staff ogling their scanned images, while concerns are mounting about subjecting children to such graphic exposure, especially after a 12-year-old girl was scanned at a Tampa airport without her parents' knowledge or consent.[4] (In Great Britain, full-body scanners are not permitted for use on children under the age of 18, and to use one for that purpose is considered a violation of child pornography laws.) And for passengers with medical implants or prostheses that may appear on scans, the procedures give rise to a whole new world of complications.

Complaints have also surfaced about travelers being subjected to retributive, harsh treatment and excessive searches when they decline a full-body scan. While screening is still optional, refusal to submit to such screenings requires a flier to endure an intrusive manual frisking by airport employees. One woman recounted that the "thorough" pat down she received after opting out of the screening was performed in a publicly embarrassing and "punitive" manner.[5]

Then there are the x-rays themselves, which have prompted concerns about their health risks. For example, David Brenner, head of Columbia University's Center for Radiological Research, asserts that x-ray scanners may emit 20 times more radiation than previously thought and may pose increased cancer risks. Radiologist Dr. Sarah Burnett warns of possible health risks to pregnant women and fetuses, while other physicians have recommended that pregnant women and children, who are the most susceptible to radiation, steer clear of the scanners altogether.

Despite the incursions into our privacy, risks to our health, and the admitted shortcoming of the scanners' inability to disclose material hidden in the groin area and body cavities, government demand for the x-ray technology remains high. Then again, if you follow the money trail, which leads straight to private corporations all too willing to exploit national security fears by peddling security technology and equipment via lobbyists and influential Washington figures, this resolute march towards a surveillance state starts to make a little more sense.

As James Ridgeway, author of *The Five Unanswered Questions About 9/11*, notes, "Airport security has always been compromised by corporate interests. When it comes to high-tech screening methods, the TSA [Transportation Security Agency] has a dismal record of enriching private corporations with failed technologies."[6] Thus, it should come as little surprise that in the days following the underwear bomber's foiled attempt, share prices for security imaging production companies skyrocketed and competition for security imaging government contracts turned into a veritable "feeding frenzy."

That barely scratches the surface of the semi-incestuous relationship between mega-corporations and the government. Still, you don't have to dig too deep to expose the seedy underbelly. The full-body scanner lobby and their private security corporation employers are a chummy group made up of former TSA personnel, as well as former members of Congress and former congressional staff. A perfect example of this is Rapiscan Systems, which retains the Chertoff Group, a security business consultant headed by former Department of Homeland Security Secretary Michael Chertoff.[7] Using the underwear bomber's failed terrorist attempt to great advantage, Chertoff almost immediately started making the rounds of various media outlets to promote Rapiscan's full-body scanners. Unless specifically asked, Chertoff did not mention his associations within the security industry— despite the fact that these associations date back to his stint in the Bush administration, when the first Rapiscan scanners were procured by the government, and have resulted in exponential pay-offs for Rapiscan. In 2009, for example, the TSA bought $25 million worth of full-body scanners from Rapiscan with finances supplied by the tax-funded American Recovery and Reinvestment Act. Ironically enough, what this means is that we the taxpayers are paying to erect our own electronic prison.

Make no mistake: Americans are not being resolutely moved into a surveillance state because some guy tried to detonate a bomb in his underwear. Obviously, these corporations, aided and abetted by the government, were waiting in the wings for some half-baked terrorist to give them a reason to spring this on us. And when that happened, corporations did not hesitate to make a killing at taxpayer expense.

And what a killing it is. The TSA initially plans to roll out a total of 450 full-body scanners, with the cost of installing the approximately $150,000-a-pop machines adding up to a whopping $67.5 million—and that's just for the devices installed in 2010. An additional $88 million is included in the 2011 national fiscal budget for 500 more machines. In order to offset the exorbitant expenditures for further security equipment purchases, some of these costs will inevitably be transferred to passengers. What this means, of course, is that the price of your airplane tickets is going up.

We've travelled a long road since 9/11. Among the many abuses we've had to endure, we've been subjected to government agents wiretapping our phones, reading our mail, monitoring our emails, and carrying out warrantless "black bag" searches of our homes. Reassured that it was for our own good and the security of the country, we let them slide.

Then we have had to deal with surveillance cameras mounted on street corners and in traffic lights, weather satellites co-opted for use as spy cameras from space, and thermal sensory imaging devices that can detect heat and movement through walls. Still we didn't really raise a fuss. By the time the government announced its plans in early 2010 to install full-body scanners in airports, we barely batted an eye, despite concerns raised about associated health risks, privacy intrusions and amplified costs. Now we're going to be subjected to these scanners patrolling our streets with government Peeping Toms watching our every move, even in our homes.

CHAPTER EIGHT

THE MARK OF THE BEAST?

"This calls for wisdom. If anyone has insight, let him calculate the number of the beast, for it is man's number. His number is 666."
—Revelation 13:18

As technology grows more sophisticated and the government and its corporate allies further refine their methods of keeping tabs on the American people, those of us who treasure privacy increasingly find ourselves engaged in a struggle to maintain our freedoms in the midst of the modern surveillance state.

Just consider the many ways we're already being monitored and tracked: through our Social Security numbers, bank accounts, purchases and electronic transactions; by way of our correspondence and communications devices—email, phone calls and mobile phones; through chips implanted in our vehicles, identification documents, even our clothing. Data corporations are capturing vast caches of personal information on you so that airports, retailers, police and other government authorities can instantly identify and track you. Add to this the fact that businesses, schools and other facilities are relying more and more on fingerprints and facial recognition to identify us. All the while, banks and other financial institutions must verify the identities of new customers and make such records of customer transactions available to the police and government officials upon request.

In recent years, this information glut has converged into a mandate for a national ID card, which came to a head with Congress' passage of the REAL ID Act in 2005. REAL ID requires states to issue machine-readable drivers' licenses containing a wealth of personal data. However, because the REAL ID Act has been opposed by many states due to its financial cost and implementation, Americans have yet to be subjected to a national ID card. That may all change depending on what happens with any immigration reform bill legislation enacted by Congress.

A centerpiece of one immigration bill as proposed by Senators Charles Schumer (D-NY) and Lindsey Graham (R-SC) is a requirement that *all* U.S. workers, citizen and resident alike, be required to obtain and carry *biometric* Social Security cards (national ID cards under a different name) in order to work within the United States. Attempting to appease critics of a national ID card, Schumer and Graham insist that "no government database would house everyone's information" and that the "cards would not contain any private information, medical information, or tracking devices."[1] However, those claims are blatantly false. Indeed, this proposed biometric card is nothing more than an end-run around opposition to a national ID card.

Civil and privacy rights advocates, as well as liberal-, conservative-, and libertarian-leaning organizations, have long raised concerns that a national ID card would enable the government to track citizens and, thus, jeopardize the privacy rights of Americans. In 1981, President Reagan likened such a proposal to the biblical "mark of the beast," and President Clinton dismissed a similar plan because it smacked of Big Brother.

At a minimum, these proposed cards will contain a memory device that stores distinct—and highly personal— physical or biological information unique to the cardholder such as fingerprints, retina scan information, a mapping of the veins on the top of your hand and so on. Eventually, other information, such as personal business and financial data, will also be stored on these cards. For the cards to be effective, an information storage system and central database, which will be managed by the government and its corporate handlers, will be required. That means millions of taxpayer dollars will be used to create the ultimate tracking device to be used against American citizens.

As journalist Megan Carpentier reported, "The federal government wants to spend hundreds of millions of dollars, and force employees and employers still suffering from a recession to do the same, to create and make accessible to every employer a national database of the fingerprints of all Americans from the time they are 14 years old.

And they want to do it in order to keep an estimated 11.9 million unauthorized immigrants—less than 4 percent of the total population of the United States—from accessing the job market."[2] Under threat of substantial fines by the government and in what promises to be a cumbersome bureaucratic process, employers will have to purchase ID card scanning devices (or visit their local Department of Motor Vehicles) in order to scan the cards of every individual they wish to hire before that individual can be employed. What this amounts to, essentially, is a troubling system in which *all* Americans would have to get clearance from the federal government in order to get a job.

Furthermore, the law's requirement that machine-readable technology be incorporated into the card opens the door for radio frequency identification (RFID) tags to be placed on the cards. RFID is a tiny, automatic identification system that enables data—in this case, the private information of American citizens—to be transmitted by a portable device. This will provide the government with unprecedented access to American citizens' personal information. In addition, RFID tags emit radio frequency signals that allow the government to track the movement of the cards, as well as the cardholders. In other words, wherever your card goes, eventually, so will the government monitors.

When all is said and done, the adoption of a national biometric ID card serves one purpose only: to provide the government with the ultimate control over the American people. If you don't possess a biometric ID card, you will not be a functioning citizen in American society. Failing to have a biometric card will render you a non-person for all intents and purposes. Your whole life will depend on this card—your ability to work, travel, buy, sell, access health care, and so on.

What we used to call science fiction is now reality. And whether a national ID card is the mark of the Beast or the long arm of Big Brother, the outcome remains the same.

CHAPTER NINE
THE GLOBAL POLICE

"The essence of Government is power; and power, lodged as it must be in human hands, will ever be liable to abuse."
—James Madison[1]

Barack Obama has shown himself to be a skillful and savvy politician. For example, in one breath, Obama pays lip service to the need for greater transparency in government, while in another, he issues executive orders that result in even more government secrecy.

Obama is aided in this Machiavellian mindset by a mainstream media seemingly loath to criticize him or scrutinize his actions too closely. A perfect example of this is the media's relative lack of scrutiny over Obama's transformation of Executive Order (EO) 12425 from a document that constitutionally limited the International Criminal Police Organization's (Interpol) activities domestically to one that established it as an autonomous police agency within the United States.

Those who voiced their concerns about this domestic empowerment of Interpol by President Obama—and that's exactly what it is—were soundly criticized for fomenting political hysteria. But there is legitimate cause for concern. This presidential directive could undermine civil liberties and render the Fourth Amendment null and void.

First, some background on EO 12425. Issued by President Ronald Reagan in 1983, EO 12425 recognized Interpol as an international organization with certain privileges and immunities afforded to foreign diplomats. However, Reagan structured his executive order to ensure that Interpol, like every other law enforcement agency in this country, was accountable to the rule of law.

Aided by some crafty legal editing, the Obama administration has manipulated Reagan's directive in such a way as to remove those restrictions so that Interpol now stands apart from domestic law enforcement agencies, its actions and records effectively immune from legal scrutiny. Shrewdly drafted, this executive order is so shrouded in the legal parsing of semicolons and redactions that it is barely comprehensible to the average citizen (unless you happen to have a few attorneys on hand who can sift through the historical record to make sense of the changes). But when you compile all the changes, the amended text of the Executive Order reads:

> Property and assets of international organizations, wherever located and by whomsoever held, shall be immune from search, unless such immunity be expressly waived, and from confiscation. The archives of international organizations shall be inviolable.[2]

The key here is the word "inviolable," which means that Interpol assets, records and other property are no longer subject to the search and seizure provisions of the Fourth Amendment, nor are they subject to public scrutiny under the Freedom of Information Act.

It should come as little surprise that when the White House issued the amended executive order on December 17, 2009, it issued no press releases and thus generated little in the way of media attention. It must be said, however, that had George W. Bush attempted to slip something like this through a week before Christmas, he would have and should have been soundly lambasted by the media.

Frankly, we should have heard more about Obama's EO 12425 from the White House and from Congress, not to mention from the media. In fact, Congress should have held hearings on the ramifications of allowing Interpol to operate within the borders of America, not only with complete autonomy but outside the strictures of the Constitution and above the rule of law.

Operating in 188 countries, Interpol supposedly deals with crimes that overlap various countries such as terrorism, organized crime, war crimes, piracy, drug trafficking, child pornography and genocide. The agency maintains a bureau in each member country and channels information and requests to the appropriate law enforcement agency in each country. It also works closely with international tribunals, such as the International Criminal Court, to locate and detain alleged fugitives.

In the U.S., Interpol is headquartered at the Justice Department in Washington, DC, one of the most powerful of government agencies and the one responsible for overseeing all law enforcement within America. All law enforcement agencies that fall under the jurisdiction of the Justice Department, including the FBI and the Drug Enforcement Agency, are subject to the rigorous safeguards of the Constitution, the Bill of Rights and the laws passed by Congress.

These safeguards no longer apply to Interpol, whose records cannot be obtained through FOIA requests—which act as an important defense against governmental abuse—nor are they subject to investigation by other federal agencies or the courts (unless Interpol itself consents).

It's difficult to know exactly what the fallout from this executive order will be, but the ramifications for the American people could be ominous. For instance, if Interpol engages in illegal and/or unconstitutional activities against American citizens, it will be impossible for U.S. citizens to obtain information—via subpoena or other commonly used legal methods—regarding its records or activities.

Additionally, any information shared by the FBI or other American intelligence agencies with Interpol will also most likely be exempt from FOIA and Fourth Amendment protections. At this point, the rule of law breaks down completely. American intelligence and police agencies, when and if they share information with Interpol, are above the law.

This also paves the way for a global police state—one in which information made available to Interpol by American agencies can and most likely will be shared with global police agencies around the world. In other words, foreign intelligence agencies now have the ability to spy on Americans.

Clearly, there are enough concerns about the impact of EO 12425 on our civil liberties to warrant further discussion. It must be remembered that James Madison, the "father" of the U.S. Constitution and the Bill of Rights and the fourth president of the United States, advised that we should "take alarm at the *first* experiment upon our liberties."[3]

Whether or not you consider President Obama's Interpol executive order to be cause for alarm, one must agree that this is far from the *first* experiment on our liberties. Indeed, the danger in all this is that a shift toward authoritarianism is underway and only small pockets of Americans realize it. Certainly, the mainstream media is not reporting on it, nor do they primarily function as watchdogs, guarding against encroachments of our rights. Yet it is unmistakable—we have been creeping towards authoritarianism for some time now, as Bertram Gross foretold many years ago. Writing in his insightful book

Friendly Fascism, he predicted, "The new fascism will be colored by national and cultural heritage, ethnic and religious composition, formal structure, and geopolitical environment." He continues:

> Anyone looking for black shirts, mass parties or men on horseback will miss the telltale clues of creeping fascism. In America, it would be supermodern and multi-ethnic—as American as Madison Avenue, executive luncheons, credit cards, and apple pie. It would be fascism with a smile. As a warning against its cosmetic façade, subtle manipulation, and velvet gloves, I call it friendly fascism. What scares me most is its subtle appeal.[4]

CHAPTER TEN

SECRET PRISONS IN AMERICA

"The very word 'secrecy' is repugnant in a free and open society; and we are as a people inherently and historically opposed to secret societies, to secret oaths, and to secret proceedings."
— John F. Kennedy[1]

How will you know that you're living in a police state? When law enforcement authorities are empowered to stop and search anyone they deem to be "suspicious," when citizens are being snatched up and made to disappear with no access to the legal system, and when it's your own government that is operating secret prisons—it's a safe bet you're under the auspices of an emerging totalitarian regime.

Do you think this couldn't happen in America? Think again. It's been happening for years under our very noses. Since 2004, for example, police officers in New York City have stopped nearly 3 million people. Incredibly, almost 90 percent of those stopped were blacks and Hispanics. Worse, these people did nothing wrong. Even so, their names have been entered into a permanent police database for use in future investigations.[2]

This type of police activity is now occurring in other places in America. And for those arrested, jail will not be their biggest worry. It's whether anyone will ever hear of them again—in other words, whether they'll be made to disappear.

Speaking at a 2008 gathering of police and sheriffs, James Pendergraph, the executive director of Immigration and Customs Enforcement's (ICE) Office of State and Local Coordination, bragged, "If you don't have enough evidence to charge someone criminally, but you think he's illegal, we can make him disappear."[3] In fact, the federal government has made countless people—including some legal residents and American citizens—"disappear" through the use of secret detention centers hidden in warehouse-like facilities in communities across America.

In an exposé for *The Nation*, law professor Jacqueline Stevens reveals that ICE is operating at least 186 such detention centers. The problem, as Stevens points out, is that "with no detention rules and being off the map spatially and otherwise, ICE agents at these locations are acting in ways that are unconscionable and unlawful." Worse, writes Stevens, concerning one such detention center known as B-18:

> If you're putting people in a warehouse, the occupants become inventory. Inventory does not need showers, beds, drinking water, soap, toothbrushes, sanitary napkins, mail, attorneys or legal information, and can withstand the constant blast of cold air. The US residents held in B-18, as many as 100 on any given day, were treated likewise. B-18, it turned out,

was not a transfer area from point A to point B but rather an irrationally revolving stockroom that would shuttle the same people briefly to the local jails, sometimes from 1 to 5 am, and then bring them back, shackled to one another, stooped and crouching in overpacked vans. These transfers made it impossible for anyone to know their location, as there would be no notice to attorneys or relatives when people moved. At times the B-18 occupants were left overnight, the frigid onslaught of forced air and lack of mattresses or bedding defeating sleep. The hours of sitting in packed cells on benches or the concrete floor meant further physical and mental duress.[4]

At the point that law enforcement officials—appointed government agents who are financed with our taxpayer dollars—are locking citizens and non-citizens away in secret prisons where they have no access to family members or attorneys, we have crossed over into a new and troubling era in the history of our nation. As Aaron Tarin, an immigration attorney in Salt Lake City, remarked, "You've got these senior agents who have all the authority in the world because they're out in the middle of nowhere. You've got rogue agents doing whatever they want. Most of the buildings are unmarked; the vehicles they drive are unmarked."[5]

Rogue agents, nondescript buildings, unmarked windowless vehicles—these are just some of the hallmarks of a secretive regime where justice is meted out gulag-style. Mark Lyttle knows first-hand how terrifying this gulag-style form of justice can be. An American citizen who suffers from bipolar disorder, speaks no Spanish and has no Mexican ancestry, Lyttle had never been outside the country. He had, however, seen the inside of a jail, and that's where his troubles began. Lyttle, who had been living in a group home, was made to serve time in jail for inappropriately touching an employee. Unfortunately for Lyttle, the jail wrongly listed his place of birth as Mexico, rather than Rowan County, N.C., where he was actually born. Unbeknownst to his family, Lyttle was handed over to ICE under the pretext that he was an illegal alien.

Shuffled around from one detention center to another, Lyttle was eventually deported to Mexico. Lacking any form of identification, it took him almost two years—all the while being forcibly shuffled from Mexico to Honduras to Nicaragua and finally to Guatemala—to make his way back to America. "We're an all-American family with two soldiers and a family member who happens to be handicapped," said Mark's brother, Brian, who serves in the U.S. Army. "It's like spitting on my uniform that you would do that to my brother."[6]

Lyttle is not alone. Hector Veloz, also a U.S. citizen, was locked in an Arizona prison for 13 months after immigration officials mistook him for an illegal immigrant. There are hundreds more like Lyttle and Veloz who are being wrongfully and unconstitutionally detained and, in some cases, deported, despite being legitimate U.S. citizens. Unfortunately, as the *San Francisco Chronicle* reports, "in immigration detention it falls to the detainees to prove their citizenship. But detainees don't have the constitutional protections, such as the right to legal counsel, that would help them prove their case." Furthermore, "immigration detainees are routinely shipped to remote jails where free legal aid is unavailable, their families are not notified of their whereabouts, and they are often denied access to telephones, mail and even medical care."[7]

Is this really the way we want our government to mete out justice? As Alison Parker, deputy director of Human Rights Watch, explains, the government should provide "an impartial authority to review the lawfulness of custody. Part and parcel is the ability of somebody to find the person and to make their presence known to a court."[8] That's why we have the habeas corpus provision in the Constitution. Latin for "bring forth the body," the Great Writ of Habeas Corpus ensures that if you're being held in a jail or prison and haven't been charged with a crime, you have the right to go before an impartial judge and ask, "Why am I being held? What is the evidence against me?"

In other words, the Writ of Habeas Corpus prevents the government from locking you up and throwing away the key. It ensures that justice is served: that the guilty are rightfully punished and the innocent are not wrongfully imprisoned and left without any recourse for gaining their freedom.

Imprisoning people and causing them to disappear was the way of the old world, and America's founders detested this practice. They believed that the right of habeas corpus was essential if American freedom and democracy were to be maintained. They fought the War of Independence in part so that the lawless capture and secret detention of prisoners would never occur again.

Alexander Hamilton, one of the more conservative of America's founding fathers, once said that the writ of habeas corpus was perhaps more important to freedom and liberty than any other right found in the Constitution. Believing that arbitrary imprisonment is "in all ages, the favorite and most formidable instrument of tyranny,"[9] the Founders were all the more determined to ensure that the people had safeguards against government abuses such as those being carried out by ICE today.

Unfortunately, in our zeal to halt the nearly one million plus illegal aliens flooding across our borders annually—an undeniable problem that needs to be resolved—we risk undermining our own rule of law and rendering our Constitution null and void. After all, if government agents can detain citizens like Mark Lyttle and Hector Veloz, what's to stop them from snatching you up and locking you away, without the ability to contact your loved ones or your lawyer?

CHAPTER ELEVEN

POLICE OVERKILL

"Soon as they hit the window, I hit the floor and went to reach for my granddaughter. I seen the light leave out of her eyes. I knew she was dead. She had blood coming out of her mouth. Lord Jesus, I ain't never seen nothing like that in my life."

—Mertilla Jones, Aiyana's grandmother[1]

It was 12:40 am on Sunday, May 16, 2010. Twenty-five-year-old Charles Jones had just gone to bed after covering his 7-year-old daughter Aiyana with her favorite blanket. The little girl was asleep on the living room sofa, which was positioned under a window. Her grandmother Mertilla was nearby. Suddenly, the silence of the night was shattered by a flash grenade thrown through the living room window, followed by the sounds of police bursting into the apartment and a gun going off. Rushing into the room, Charles found himself tackled by police and forced to lie on the floor, his face in a pool of blood. His daughter Aiyana's blood.[2]

It would be hours before Charles would be informed that his daughter was dead. According to news reports, the little girl was shot in the neck by the lead officer's gun after he collided with Aiyana's grandmother during a police raid gone awry. The 34-year-old suspect the police had been looking for would later be found elsewhere during a search of the building. Ironically, a camera crew shadowing the police SWAT team for the reality television show "The First 48" caught the unfolding tragedy on film.[3]

As far-fetched as what happened to the Joneses may sound, they are not the only American family to suffer the devastating consequences of a police raid gone awry. According to Radley Balko's *Overkill: The Rise of Paramilitary Police Raids in America* (2006), over 40,000 SWAT team raids are carried out annually in this country, striking at the very core of our constitutional freedoms. As Balko writes, "There's an old Cold War saying commonly attributed to Winston Churchill...that goes, 'Democracy means that when there's a knock on the door at 3 a.m., it's probably the milkman.' The idea is that free societies don't send armed government agents dressed in black to raid the private homes of citizens for political crimes."[4]

Regrettably, we live in an age where police raids are on the rise, modern police surveillance is more invasive than ever, and the government has unfettered access to the most private matters of our lives. Thus, the reality we must contend with is one in which the Fourth Amendment, which guarantees essential privacy rights such as the right to be free from unreasonable searches or seizures by the government, is on life support. Yet those who drafted the

Bill of Rights, the first ten amendments to the Constitution, considered freedom in one's home the most essential liberty.

Deeply concerned about preserving personal liberty and property rights, the Framers believed those rights to be of paramount importance—even over public safety. In such an environment, citizens were seen as equals with law enforcement officials, and authorities were almost never permitted to enter one's home without permission. Modern SWAT team raids where the police crash into the homes of Americans would have been seen as the essence of tyranny. Indeed, it was not uncommon for police officers to be held personally liable for trespass when they wrongfully invaded a citizen's home. And unlike today, early Americans would resist arrest when a police officer tried to restrain them without a proper justification or warrant—which they had a right to read before being arrested.

This clear demand for a right to privacy stemmed from a deep-seated distrust of those in power and their potential to abuse the authority entrusted to them by the citizenry. Over time, however, that instinctive distrust of government has given way to a false sense of security rooted in the belief that the government is looking out for our best interests. Thus, as our complacency about the need to actively and personally defend our freedoms has increased, the government's commitment to respecting our Fourth Amendment rights has dissipated.

To our detriment, Americans today seem more attuned to what's happening on trendy reality TV shows than the goings-on in their federal government. Distracted by their gadgets and caught up in their virtual communities, many Americans have failed to notice what's happening in their own backyards—with the transformation of law enforcement officials into paramilitary police forces being one of the most alarming developments in recent years. As Balko points out, "Today, every decent-sized city has a SWAT team, and most have several. Even absurdly small towns like Eufaula, Ala., (population 13,463) have them... Where their purpose once was to defuse an already violent situation, today they break into homes to look for illicit drugs, creating violence and confrontation where there was none before."[5]

While we're fortunate to have many law enforcement agents who strive to honor and respect the Constitution, to our misfortune, we have failed to raise objections to the mixed messages being sent when those same agents are sent to patrol our communities dressed as storm troopers, equipped with invasive technologies and sophisticated weaponry, and authorized to use military tactics in their efforts to uphold the law. In fact, even the equipment used by police during routine traffic stops, such as sophisticated flashlights containing super-sensitive detectors that sense the contents of your breath, has contributed to the steady erosion of our freedoms. Despite our having a constitutional right to privacy and to not be subjected to unreasonable searches, police conspicuously situate these devices in front of our faces and into our personal space, and we are left with no say in the matter.

Unfortunately, the U.S. Supreme Court has been a willing accomplice in this depreciation of our essential liberties, handing down rulings that provide the government with endless ways to pervert the letter and spirit of the Fourth Amendment. Such rulings, issued in the name of so-called police safety, national security and citizen protection, have given rise to language the Framers never foresaw nor intended, such as protective sweep exception, hot pursuit exception, inevitable discovery exception and good faith exception, to name just a few.

Yet there are some things which no decent human being can remain silent about. Americans should be outraged when police officers use tasers on defenseless children,[6] autistic teenagers,[7] pregnant women[8] and senior citizens[9]—all incidents that have been in the news in recent years. We should be up in arms over what happened to young Aiyana Jones in Detroit. No family should have to suffer the loss of a child because police officers got carried away during a SWAT team raid. And no community should feel threatened by the presence of law enforcement officials patrolling their streets.

Where does this leave us? Having largely relinquished control over our liberties and our lives to the government, we have come to something of an impasse in terms of our freedoms. The only way forward, especially if we are to revive our ailing Fourth Amendment and restore the balance of power between citizen and government, is to reclaim our rightful sovereignty over our possessions and our lives. That is easier said than done, however. As history shows, power, once handed over to the government, is not easily wrested back.

CHAPTER TWELVE
THE GROUNDWORK HAS BEEN LAID FOR MARTIAL LAW

In the councils of government, we must guard against the acquisition of unwarranted influence, whether sought or unsought, by the military-industrial complex. The potential for the disastrous rise of misplaced power exists and will persist. We must never let the weight of this combination endanger our liberties or democratic processes. We should take nothing for granted.

—Dwight D. Eisenhower[1]

During his two terms in office, George W. Bush stepped outside the boundaries of the Constitution and assembled an amazing toolbox of powers that greatly increased the authority of the president and the reach of the federal government.

Bush expanded presidential power to, among other things, allow government agents to secretly open the private mail of American citizens; authorize government agents to secretly, and illegally, listen in on the phone calls of American citizens and read our e-mails; assume control of the federal government following a "catastrophic event"; and declare martial law.

Thus, the groundwork was laid for an imperial presidency and a potentially totalitarian government—a state of affairs that has not ended with Barack Obama's ascension to the Oval Office, despite hopes to the contrary that President Obama would fully restore the balance between government and its citizens to a pre-Bush status quo. As Charlie Savage reports in the *New York Times*, "Signs suggest that the administration's changes may turn out to be less sweeping than many had hoped or feared— prompting growing worry among civil liberties groups and a sense of vindication among supporters of Bush-era policies."[2]

The fact is that the problem is bigger than Obama or any individual who occupies the White House. Once the government assumes expansive powers and crosses certain constitutional lines, it's almost impossible to pull back.

Just consider some of the lines that have already been crossed. The local police, as we have seen, have already evolved into *de facto* extensions of the military. Dressed as Darth Vader look-alikes, the police have opted for the SWAT-team dress formally adopted by the federal agencies. Congressional legislation allows the U.S. military, by way of the Pentagon, to train civilian police. The Pentagon has also provided local police with military equipment such as M-16 rifles, bayonets, boats, vehicles, surveillance equipment, chemical suits and flak jackets, among other items. Thus, the local police are armed to the teeth.

We already have a federal police force comprised of numerous governmental agencies that coordinate with local police, who are authorized to carry firearms and make arrests.[3] An incident that occurred in Oklahoma demonstrates the increased and immediate involvement of federal agents in local matters with the assistance of local police. Chip Harrison, a construction worker, was pulled over by local police because of an anti-Obama sign proclaiming "Abort Obama, not the unborn" in his pickup truck window. The sign was confiscated by local police, and Harrison was informed that the sign could be considered a threat to the president. The local police contacted the Secret Service, who, within a matter of hours, came to Harrison's home and investigated the matter.[4] So much for the freedom of expression.

Now, according to the *Army Times*, we have at least 20,000 U.S. military troops deployed within our borders to "help with civil unrest and crowd control or to deal with potentially horrific scenarios such as massive poisoning and chaos in response to a chemical, biological, radiological, nuclear or high-yield explosive, or CBRNE, attack."[5] I am not alone in believing that we are just one incident away—be it a terrorist attack, a major financial blowout or a widespread natural disaster—from martial law being declared in this country (or at least sections thereof). And once that happens, the Constitution and Bill of Rights will be suspended and what government officials believe and do, no matter how arbitrary, will become law.

Our methods of communication, including the internet, are already being monitored—and, in some instances, shut down, abetted by the telecommunications giants, which act as extensions of the government. Thus, not only does the government have the ability to read our emails and open and read our personal mail, it can also listen in on our phone calls and jam our cell phone calls. As the *Washington Post* reports, federal authorities already have the ability to jam cell phones and other wireless devices. Unbeknownst to the nearly two million people who attended the Obama Inauguration festivities, federal authorities jammed cell phone signals at specific locations.[6] Such disruptions simply appear to be dropped calls or lost signals. Although jamming is technically illegal for state and local agencies, such jamming could be conducted on a more extensive basis nationwide. This would prevent citizens from being able to communicate with one another or make appeals to their government representatives.

As we have seen, we already live in a surveillance state. There was a time when people could flee when the government got out of control. Now, with our every movement monitored by cameras on sidewalks, streets and ATMs, in shops, offices, schools and parks, there truly is nowhere to hide. Moreover, equipped with high-powered satellites and massive databases, the government can track us using our cell phones, cars, credit cards, driver's licenses and passports.

For those who have been paying attention, such as former Pulitzer prize-winning war correspondent Chris Hedges, it's clear that the groundwork for a seamless transition into martial law under a totalitarian state of government has been laid. And local law enforcement, which has already been serving as a *de facto* military force, will be the key to maintaining martial law under a police state. Given the interconnectedness of our federal, state and local governmental agencies, you can be sure that all of this will happen quickly.

All that is needed is another threat to national security—a so-called "catastrophic event." Under the Bush administration, the danger was terrorism. Under the Obama administration, the economy is being posed as the greatest threat to national security.

This danger was made clear in a U.S. Army War College report issued in the fall of 2008. As Chris Hedges reports, "The military must be prepared, the document warned, for a 'violent, strategic dislocation inside the United States,' which could be provoked by 'unforeseen economic collapse,' 'purposeful domestic resistance,' 'pervasive public health emergencies' or 'loss of functioning political and legal order.' The 'widespread civil violence,' the document said, 'would force the defense establishment to reorient priorities in extremis to defend basic domestic order and human security.'"[7]

What does all this mean for you and me, the average citizen? When and if martial law is declared, freedom, as we have known it, will be obsolete. And don't expect much in the way of warning or help from the corporate media. As the wars in Iraq and Afghanistan show, the media is all too willing to be co-opted by the military for the sake of access and ratings.

PART TWO

"Unless we teach the ideas that make America a miracle of government, it will go away in your kids' lifetimes, and we will be a fable. You have to find the time and creativity to teach it in schools, and if you don't, you will lose it. You will lose it to the darkness, and what this country represents is a tiny twinkle of light in a history of oppression and darkness and cruelty. If it lasts for more than our lifetime, for more than our kids' lifetime, it is only because we put some effort into teaching what it is, the ideas of America: the idea of opportunity, mobility, freedom of thought, freedom of assembly."

—Richard Dreyfuss, Oscar-winning actor and civics education activist, on *The Bill Maher Show*, Nov. 26, 2006

CHAPTER THIRTEEN
WILL OUR FREEDOMS SURVIVE?

> *"A millennium hence America will be hard to recognize. It may not exist as a nation-state in the form it does now— or even exist at all. Will the transitions ahead be gradual and peaceful or abrupt and catastrophic? Will our descendants be living productive lives in a society better than the one we inhabit now? Whatever happens, will valuable aspects of America's legacy weave through the fabric of civilizations to come? Will historians someday have reason to ask, Did America really fall?"*
>
> —Cullen Murphy[1]

I have seen the new face of America, and it is troubling. According to an expansive study by the Pew Research Center in 2010, the Millennial generation is the so-called "new face of America."[2] Comprised of 50 million young people between the ages of 18-29, the Millennials have been so dubbed because they are the first generation to come of age in the new millennium. However, the study, which aims to shed light on what America might be like in the future, raises some provocative questions about this up-and-coming generation of citizens and leaders and what they might mean for the future of our nation.

For example, Millennials are "less religious, less likely to have served in the military, and are on track to become the most educated generation in American history. Their entry into careers and first jobs has been badly set back by the Great Recession, but they are more upbeat than their elders about their own economic futures as well as about the overall state of the nation."[3]

This group of tweens and twenty-somethingers is also history's first "always connected" generation. Yet as the report points out, what really sets the Millennials apart is not merely their exceptional use of technological gadgets but the manner in which they've fused their social lives into them. "Steeped in digital technology and social media, they treat their multi-tasking hand-held gadgets almost like a body part—for better and worse. More than eight-in-ten say they sleep with a cell phone glowing by the bed, poised to disgorge texts, phone calls, emails, songs, news, videos, games and wake-up jingles."[4]

And while many Americans are concerned with freedom, civil liberties and the encroaching government, it seems as if the next generation is primarily concerned with the freedom to be on their gadgets. According to Pew, although two-thirds of Millennials say "you can't be too careful" when dealing with people, they are less skeptical than their elders of government. They (41%) are also more satisfied than their elders with the way things are going in the country.

Yet with everyone from the right to the left talking about how bad things are in this country—we're moving into a surveillance state, unemployment is skyrocketing, increasing numbers of children are in poverty, people are losing their homes, and the country is on the verge of economic collapse—how could a generation that has had more access to information and education think the state of the nation is pretty good?

First of all, this is one of the first generations to come of age that was completely institutionalized. From daycare through college, they have spent most of their waking hours away from their homes. Locked away in unreal environments, they've generally been pampered and shielded from what's happening in the real world—a world filled with corruption, greed, murder, chaos and mayhem.

Second, they are a narcissistic generation with an overblown sense of entitlement. As *Newsweek* writer Raina Kelly observed, "we've built up the confidence of our kids, but in that process, we've created a generation of hot-house flowers puffed with a disproportionate sense of self-worth (the definition of narcissism) and without the resiliency skills they need when Mommy and Daddy can't fix something."[5] Used to having someone else solve their problems for them, it should come as no surprise that more than half (53%) of Millennials believe government should do more to solve problems. That's just a short step away from a compliant citizenry that allows the government to call the shots.

Third, the Millennials have been exposed to an educational system lacking in the basic rudiments of education as it's been classically understood. Although they may know more about math and science than previous generations, they know very little about their own history, their Constitution, or their rights. Studies show that only a small percentage even know that Thomas Jefferson wrote the Declaration of Independence or that George Washington was the first president. Very few of them are even acquainted with the great struggles of history such as the American civil rights movement. And virtually none of them have even read the basic freedom writings of Martin Luther King, Jr. I would venture to say that the greatest disservice done to this generation has come through the educational system and its imposition of mind-numbing conformity, beginning with draconian zero tolerance policies in middle and high schools, through political correctness in modern universities.

Fourth, although the Pew survey shows them to be the "always connected" generation, upon closer examination, it would seem that the Millennials are not so much *connected* to their technologies as they are *addicted*. They're generally consumed with themselves and not the world around them, a behavior reinforced by technology, which reduces the world to you and your hand-held inanimate object of choice, whether it be a cell phone, an iPod or a laptop computer.

Fifth, it would be more apt to describe the Millennials as the disconnected generation. Physically in the world, they are lacking in community, mentally alienated from each other, unable to reach out to other people in any meaningful, intimate fashion. There will come a time when you walk into a family room and each family member will be in their own world, with their own ear buds, in a virtual world of their own making.

Sixth, the Millennials are oblivious to much of what is going on around them as far as current events, public policy and world affairs. Then again, it's almost impossible to stay well-informed by watching television, because television packages everything—including the so-called "news shows"—in the form of entertainment. Thus, raised in front of television screens and computer video game consoles, this generation is accustomed to being entertained—a service largely provided by the internet today. While previous generations received their basic information from newspapers and books, this generation tends to surf the internet. But as studies show, internet readers generally read those things they agree with and are lost in trivia like Facebook. In other words, they're not avidly studying opposing points of view and thus learning to think critically and analytically.

This is not to say that all Millennials are disconnected and oblivious. But collectively, they're shaping up to be a generation of compliant, uninformed citizens who will be inclined to go along with most things as long as the corporate state can keep them happily hooked to their gadgets.

We have come to a crossroads generationally. We've lost our identity as a people and as a country, and the Millennial generation has no idea who they are. The torch will soon be passed to the next generation. If the trends continue as they have, I fear that the Millennial generation will be a lost generation, and freedom as we have known it will be lost as well.

CHAPTER FOURTEEN

TEACHING TOTALITARIANISM

"Censorship reflects society's lack of confidence in itself. It is a hallmark of an authoritarian regime."

—U.S. Supreme Court Justice Potter Stewart[1]

Why are many Americans so willing to hand over their rights at the first sign of unrest or disturbance? The reason is simple yet troubling: Americans have come to view freedom as expedient and expendable because that's what they've been taught.

Over the past several decades, America's public schools have increasingly adopted the mindset that students have little, if no, rights and school officials have not been reticent about communicating this message to young people. Moreover, this totalitarian outlook has been reinforced by an educational curriculum so focused on preparing students to enter the machinery of the corporate state that there is little time left over for the things they really need to learn, such as what their rights are, how to exercise them and the duties and responsibilities of citizenship. As a result, the majority of students today have little knowledge of the freedoms enshrined in the Constitution and, specifically, in the Bill of Rights.

For example, a national survey of high school students reveals that only 2% can identify the Chief Justice of the Supreme Court; 35% know that "We the people" are the first three words of the U.S. Constitution; 1.8% know that James Madison is considered the father of the U.S. Constitution; and 25% know that the Fifth Amendment protects against double jeopardy and self incrimination, among other legal rights.[2]

Public educators do not fare much better in understanding and implementing the Constitution in the classroom.[3] A study conducted by the University of Connecticut found that while public educators seem to support First Amendment rights in principle, they are reluctant to apply such rights in the schools.[4] Consequently, the few students who do know and exercise their rights are forced to deal with school officials who, more often than not, refuse to respect those rights.

Two incidents that happened in 2010 illustrate how bad things have gotten in the schools:

School officials at Albemarle High School in Charlottesville, Va.—ironically enough, the much-vaunted home of Thomas Jefferson—ordered the destruction of an eight-page edition of their student newspaper which had already been printed and was awaiting distribution. Why? Because school officials feared that an editorial questioning whether student-athletes need gym class might upset PE teachers. The newspaper, dubiously named *The Revolution*, was subsequently reprinted minus the editorial.[5]

In Norfolk, Va., two teachers at Norview High School were placed on administrative leave for distributing "unauthorized" materials to their 12th grade government students. The materials, a one-page handout and a video, advised the students about how to deal with police if stopped. Specifically, the materials explain how legal rights apply to police searches of vehicles, homes or individuals and how people can cite those rights during encounters with police.[6]

These two situations barely scratch the surface regarding the hostile nature of today's public school environment, at least in terms of individuality and freedom. For the nearly 50 million students who are attending elementary and secondary public schools, their time in school will be marked by overreaching zero tolerance policies, heightened security and surveillance and a greater emphasis on conformity and behavior-controlling drugs— all either aimed at or resulting in the destruction of privacy and freedom. In fact, as director Cevin Soling documents in his insightful, award-winning documentary *The War on Kids* (2009)[7], the moment many young people walk into school, they find themselves under constant surveillance: they are photographed, fingerprinted, scanned, x-rayed, sniffed and snooped on. Between metal detectors at the entrances, drug-sniffing dogs in the hallways and surveillance cameras in the classrooms and elsewhere, many American schools have come to resemble prison-like complexes. Add to this the fact that young people today are immersed in a drug culture—one manufactured by the pharmaceutical industry—almost from the moment they are born, and you have the makings of a perfect citizenry for the Orwellian society in which we now live: one that can be easily cowed, controlled and directed.

In this way, with the government's power rapidly increasing while that of the individual is subject to all manner of restrictions, the public schools are a perfect microcosm of what is happening across the nation. And while the notion of free speech remains enshrined in the First Amendment of our Constitution, censorship—once considered taboo in our freedom-loving culture—is no longer a dirty word. Instead, it is what so-called responsible adults must now do in order to ensure that no one is offended or made to feel inferior.

Yet not too long ago, no one would have thought twice about teachers actually *teaching* the Bill of Rights or students exercising their free speech rights in a written editorial. Today, such acts are looked upon as radical—even revolutionary. Unfortunately, by teaching such a sinister conformity, school officials are raising up a generation of compliant, unquestioning citizens who will march in lockstep with whatever their government dictates.

CHAPTER FIFTEEN

WHY AREN'T SCHOOLS TEACHING OUR CHILDREN THEIR RIGHTS AND FREEDOMS?

"Whenever the people are well-informed, they can be trusted with their own government."
—Thomas Jefferson[1]

According to President Barack Obama, making school days longer and extending the academic school year will increase learning and raise test scores among American children. However, it's not the length of the school year that is the problem so much as the quality of education being imparted to young people, especially when it comes to knowing American history and their rights—what we used to call civics.

Clearly, the public schools are fostering civic ignorance. For example, a 2009 study of 1000 Oklahoma high school students found that only 3% would be able to pass the U.S. Immigration Services' citizenship exam, while incredibly 93% of immigrants from foreign countries who took the same test passed. In the same survey, only 28% of Oklahoma students could name the "supreme law of the land" (the Constitution), while even fewer could identify Thomas Jefferson as the author of the Declaration of Independence. Barely one out of every four students knew that George Washington was the nation's first president. None of the students correctly answered 8 or more of the 10 questions, and 97% scored 50% or less.[2]

This problem is not limited simply to Oklahoma students. It's a national problem. For example, a similar study in Arizona found that only 3.5% of public high school students would be able to pass the citizenship test, a figure not significantly exceeded by the passing rates of charter and private school students, at 7 and 14%, respectively.[3]

A survey of American adults by the American Civic Literacy Program resulted in some equally disheartening findings. Seventy-one percent failed the citizenship test. Moreover, having a college education does very little to increase civic knowledge, as demonstrated by the abysmal 32% pass rate of people holding not just a bachelor's degree but some sort of graduate-level degree.[4]

Those who drafted the U.S. Constitution understood that the only way to guarantee that freedom would survive in the new republic was through an informed citizenry—one educated on basic rights and freedoms. As Thomas Jefferson wrote, "I know no safe depository of the ultimate powers of the society but the people themselves; and if we think them not enlightened enough to exercise their control with a wholesome discretion, the remedy is not to take it from them, but to inform their discretion by education."[5]

Unfortunately, as the aforementioned surveys indicate, most Americans are constitutionally illiterate, and our young people are not much better. Despite the millions of taxpayer dollars spent on education, American public schools do a poor job of teaching the basic freedoms guaranteed in the Constitution and the Bill of Rights. Indeed, the major emphasis in public education today is on math and science. Yet even in those subjects, American students lag far behind when compared to students in other countries.

We would do well to heed Jefferson's advice on the subject of public education. He believed that pre-university education was to "instruct the mass of our citizens in… their rights, interests, and duties as men and citizens."[6] As for university education, Jefferson said it was "to form the statesmen, legislators and judges on whom public prosperity and individual happiness are so much to depend."[7]

Clearly, the ramifications of raising up untold generations of young people who are constitutionally illiterate are serious and far-reaching. These young people will be our future voters and political leaders. By failing to educate them, educators have not only done us a disservice but our nation as well.

So what's the solution?

Instead of forcing children to become part of the machinery of society by an excessive emphasis on math and science in the schools, they should be prepared to experience the beauty of becoming responsible citizens. This will mean teaching them their rights and urging them to exercise their freedoms to the fullest.

Some critics are advocating that students pass the United States citizenship exam in order to graduate from high school. Others recommend that it must be a prerequisite for attending college. I'd go so far as to argue that students should have to pass the citizenship exam before graduating from grade school.

The federal bureaucracy lodged in Washington, DC, is out of control. Increasingly, under George W. Bush, the federal government disregarded the Constitution and systematically violated the civil liberties of American citizens on a mass scale. Unfortunately, Barack Obama is continuing a similar pattern.

And whose fault is it? When I was a child going to school, I was taught American history and how radical the American founders were. I was required to take civics courses, and I knew the Bill of Rights. By the time I entered college, I was protesting government encroachment of our freedoms and liberties.

I was also taught that if students didn't learn, it's because teachers didn't teach. The unfortunate danger we now face is a government no longer controlled by the people and which no longer feels responsible toward them. This is a problem created, in part, by the educational system, but it is one that could be remedied by it as well.

PART THREE

"Few will have the greatness to bend history, but each of us can work to change a small portion of the events, and then the total—all of these acts—will be written in the history of this generation. Thousands of Peace Corps volunteers are making a difference in the isolated villages and the city slums of dozens of countries. Thousands of unknown men and women in Europe resisted the occupation of the Nazis and many died, but all added to the ultimate strength and freedom of their countries. It is from numberless diverse acts of courage and belief that human history is thus shaped. Each time a man stands up for an ideal, or acts to improve the lot of others, or strikes out against injustice, he sends forth a tiny ripple of hope, and crossing each other from a million different centers of energy and daring, those ripples build a current which can sweep down the mightiest walls of oppression and resistance."

> —Robert F. Kennedy, "Day of Affirmation Address," University of Capetown, South Africa (June 6, 1966)

CHAPTER SIXTEEN
SEVEN PRINCIPLES FOR FREE GOVERNMENT

*"The People are the only sure reliance
for the preservation of our liberty."*
—Thomas Jefferson[1]

Precisely because Americans are easily distracted—because, as study after study shows, they are clueless about their rights—and because the nation's schools have ceased teaching the fundamentals of the Constitution and the Bill of Rights—the American governmental scheme is sliding ever closer toward authoritarianism. This is taking place with little more than a whimper from an increasingly compliant populace that, intentionally or not, has allowed itself to be brainwashed into trusting politicians and their government.

If the people have little or no knowledge of the basics of government and their rights, those who wield governmental power will inevitably wield it excessively. After all, a citizenry can only hold its government accountable if it knows when the government oversteps its bounds.

The following seven principles—ones that every American should know—undergird the American system of government and form the basis for the freedoms our forefathers fought and died for. They are a good starting point for understanding what free government is really all about.

First, the maxim that *power corrupts* is an absolute truth. Realizing this, those who drafted the Constitution and the Bill of Rights held one principle sacrosanct: a distrust of all who hold governmental power. As James Madison, author of the Bill of Rights, proclaimed, "All men having power ought to be distrusted to a certain degree."[2] Moreover, in questions of power, Thomas Jefferson warned, "Let no more be heard of confidence in man, but bind him down from mischief by the chains of the Constitution."[3]

The second principle (one that has largely been turned on its head over the past several decades) is that *governments primarily exist to secure rights*, an idea that is central to constitutionalism. In appointing the government as the guardian of the people's rights, the people only give it certain enumerated powers, which are laid out in a written constitution. The idea of a written constitution actualizes the two great themes of the Declaration of Independence: consent of the governed and protection of equal rights. Thus, the purpose of constitutionalism is to limit governmental power and ensure that the government performs its basic function: to preserve and protect our rights, especially our unalienable rights to life, liberty and the pursuit of happiness, and our civil liberties.

The third principle revolves around the belief that no

one is above the law, not even those who make the law. This is termed *rule of law*. Richard Nixon's statement, "When the President does it, that means it is not illegal,"[4] would have been anathema to the Framers of the Constitution. If all people possess equal rights, the people who live under the laws must be allowed to participate in making those laws. By that same token, those who make the laws must live under the laws they make.

Separation of powers ensures that no single authority is entrusted with all the powers of government. People are not perfect, whether they are in government or out of it. As history makes clear, those in power tend to abuse it. The government is thus divided into three co-equal branches: legislative, executive and judicial. Placing all three powers in the same branch of government was considered the very definition of tyranny.

A system of *checks and balances*, essential if a constitutional government is to succeed, strengthens the separation of powers and prevents legislative despotism. Such checks and balances include dividing Congress into two houses, with different constituencies, term lengths, sizes and functions; granting the president a limited veto power over congressional legislation; and appointing an independent judiciary capable of reviewing ordinary legislation in light of the written Constitution, which is referred to as "judicial review." The Framers feared that Congress could abuse its powers and potentially emerge as the tyrannous branch because it had the power to tax. But they did not anticipate the emergence of presidential powers as they have come to dominate modern government or the inordinate influence of corporate powers on governmental decision-making.

Representation allows the people to have a voice in government by sending elected representatives to do their bidding while avoiding the need for each and every citizen to vote on every issue considered by government. In a country as large as the United States, it is not feasible to have direct participation in governmental affairs. Hence, we have a representative government. If the people don't agree with how their representatives are conducting themselves, they can and should vote them out.

Federalism is yet another constitutional device to limit the power of government by dividing power and, thus, preventing tyranny. In America, the levels of government generally break down into federal, state and local branches (which further divide into counties and towns or cities). Because local and particular interests differ from place to place, such interests are better handled at a more intimate level by local governments, not a bureaucratic national government. Remarking on the benefits of the American tradition of local self-government in the 1830s, the French historian Alexis de Tocqueville observed:

Local institutions are to liberty what primary schools are to science; they put it within the people's reach; they teach people to appreciate its peaceful enjoyment and accustom them to make use of it. Without local institutions a nation may give itself a free government, but it has not got the spirit of liberty.[5]

These seven vital principles have been largely forgotten, obscured by the haze of a centralized government, a citizenry that no longer thinks analytically, and schools that don't adequately teach our young people about their history and their rights. Yet here's the rub: while Americans wander about oblivious in their brainwashed states, their "government of the people, by the people and for the people" is being taken away from them.

The answer: get *un*-brainwashed. Learn your rights. Stand up for the founding principles. Make your voice and your vote count. If need be, vociferously protest the erosion of your freedoms at the local and national level. Most of all, do these things today. Tomorrow will most likely be too late.

CHAPTER SEVENTEEN

KNOW YOUR RIGHTS OR YOU WILL LOSE THEM

> *"It astonishes me to find...[that so many] of our countrymen...should be contented to live under a system which leaves to their governors the power of taking from them the trial by jury in civil cases, freedom of religion, freedom of the press, freedom of commerce, the habeas corpus laws, and of yoking them with a standing army. This is a degeneracy in the principles of liberty...which I [would not have expected for at least] four centuries."*
>
> —Thomas Jefferson[1]

"Most citizens," writes columnist Nat Hentoff, "are largely uneducated about their own constitutional rights and liberties."[2]

The following true incident is a case in point for Hentoff's claim. A young attorney, preparing to address a small gathering about the need to protect freedom, especially in the schools, wrote the text of the First Amendment on a blackboard. After carefully reading the text, a woman in the audience approached the attorney, pointed to the First Amendment on the board and remarked, "My, the law is really changing. Is this new?" The woman was a retired schoolteacher.

For more than 200 years, Americans have enjoyed the freedoms of speech, assembly and religion, among others, without ever really studying the source of those liberties, found in the Bill of Rights—the first ten amendments to our U.S. Constitution.

Yet never has there been a time when knowing our rights has been more critical and safeguarding them more necessary. Particularly telling is the fact that even under the Obama presidency, most of the Bush administration policies and laws that curtailed our freedoms have remained intact— all of which have drastically altered the landscape of our liberties.

Thus, it is vital that we gain a better understanding of what Thomas Jefferson described as "fetters against doing evil." If not, I fear that with each passing day, what Jefferson called the "degeneracy" of "the principles of liberty" will grow worse until, half asleep, Americans will lose what our forefathers fought and died for.

A short summary of the first ten amendments shows how vital these freedoms are.

The *First Amendment* protects the freedom to speak your mind and protest in peace without being bridled by the government. It also protects the freedom of the media, as well as the right to worship and pray without interference. In other words, Americans cannot be silenced by the government.

The *Second Amendment* guarantees "the right of the people to keep and bear arms." This is one of the most controversial provisions of the Bill of Rights. Indeed, there are those who claim that gun ownership in America should be restricted solely to the police and other government officials. In many countries, owning a firearm is a mere privilege, reserved for the rich and powerful. Self-protection, however, is not a privilege in America. It is an individual citizen right which the U.S. Supreme Court has now recognized.

America was born during a time of martial law. British troops stationed themselves in homes and entered property without regard for the rights of the owners. That is why the *Third Amendment* prohibits the military from entering any citizen's home without "the consent of the owner." Even though today's military does not yet threaten private property, this amendment reinforces the principle that civilian-elected officials are superior to the military. But increasingly, even under the Obama presidency, the threat of martial law being imposed is a clear and present danger.

There's a knock at the door. The police charge in and begin searching your home. They invade your privacy, rummaging through your belongings. You may think you're powerless to stop them, but you're not. The *Fourth Amendment* prohibits the government from searching your home without a warrant approved by a judge. But what about other kinds of invasions? Your telephone, mail, emails, computer and medical records are now subject to governmental search. Even though they're all personal and private, they are increasingly at risk for unwarranted intrusion by government agents. The ominous rise of the surveillance state threatens the protections given us by this amendment.

You cannot be tried again after having been found innocent. The government cannot try you repeatedly for the same crime, hoping to get the result they want. It's one of the legal protections of the *Fifth Amendment*. Moreover, you cannot be forced to testify against yourself. You can "plead the Fifth." This means that if you are accused of committing a crime, it is up to the state to prove its case against you. You are innocent until proven guilty, and government authorities cannot deprive you of your life, your liberty or your property without following strict legal codes of conduct.

The *Sixth Amendment* spells out the right to a "speedy and public trial." An accused person can confront the witnesses against him and demand to know the nature of the charge. The government cannot legally keep someone in jail for unspecified offenses. Moreover, unlike many other countries, Americans also have the right to be tried by a jury of ordinary citizens and to be represented by an attorney. Our fates in criminal proceedings are not decided by panels of judges or unaccountable politicians.

Property ownership is a fundamental right of free

people. In a legal dispute over property, the *Seventh Amendment* guarantees citizens the right to a jury trial.

Like any other American citizen, those accused of being criminals have rights under the Constitution as well. In some countries, the government abuses what they see as disloyal or troublesome citizens by keeping them in jail indefinitely on trumped-up charges. If they cannot pay their bail, then they're not released. The *Eighth Amendment* is, thus, similar to the Sixth—it protects the rights of the accused. These are often the people most susceptible to abuse and who have the least resources to defend themselves. This amendment also forbids the use of cruel and unusual punishment.

The framers of our Constitution were so concerned about civil liberties that they wished to do everything conceivable to protect our future freedom. Some of the framers opposed a bill of rights because it might appear that these were the only rights the people possessed. The *Ninth Amendment* remedied that by providing that other rights not listed were nonetheless retained by the people. Our rights are inherently ours, and our government was created to protect them. The government does not, nor did it ever, have the power to grant us our rights. Popular sovereignty—the belief that the power to govern flows upward from the people rather than downward from the rulers—is clearly evident in this amendment and is a landmark of American freedom.

Ours is a federal system of government. This means that power is divided among local, state and national entities. The *Tenth Amendment* reminds the national government that the people and the states retain every authority that is not otherwise mentioned in the Constitution. Congress and the President have increasingly assumed more power than the Constitution grants them. However, it's up to the people and the state governments to make sure that they obey the law of the land.

Having stood the test of time, there is little doubt that the Bill of Rights is the greatest statement for freedom ever drafted and put into effect. In the end, however, it is the vigilance of "we the people" that will keep the freedoms we hold so dear alive. Therefore, know your rights, exercise them freely or you're going to lose them.

CHAPTER EIGHTEEN

WHAT KIND OF REVOLUTIONARY WILL YOU BE?

"We know through painful experience that freedom is never voluntarily given up by the oppressor; it must be demanded by the oppressed."

—Martin Luther King, Jr.[1]

With the government's relentless assault on our pocketbooks and freedoms, the economic and fiscal picture for many Americans is bleak. The national debt is in the trillions. People are losing their homes and jobs, and millions have fallen into poverty. At the same time, lucrative tax breaks exist for the corporate rich, while the average citizen is heavily taxed. The Constitution and civil liberties have been undermined at every step. And don't expect any of these developments to let up anytime soon.

Understandably, many are bewildered. But now is not the time to shrink from our responsibility as citizens. In fact, we should welcome the chance to regain control of a government out of control. And if there is to be any change, it is going to be brought about by us, "we the people," not the politicians. No president, no congressman and no judge can do what you can.

There is no better time to act than the present. Fear,

apathy, escapism or reliance on some government official to save us will not carry the day. It is within our power as citizens to make a difference and seek corrective measures. That principle is the basis of the American governmental scheme.

We need to think like revolutionaries. Thus, there can be no room for timidity or lukewarm emotions. What we need is passion, dedication and courage. And to paraphrase Martin Luther King, Jr., we have to demand change from the oppressors.

There are certain things that are common to every successful struggle. Here are a few suggestions.[2]

Get educated. Without knowledge, very little can be accomplished. Thus, you must know your rights. Take time to read the Constitution. Study and understand history because the tales of those who seek power and those who resist it is an age-old one. Understand the vital issues of the day so that you can be cognizant of the threats to freedom.

Get involved. Become actively involved in community affairs, politics and legal battles. Think nationally, but act locally. If our freedoms are to be restored, taking action at that local level must be the starting point. Getting involved in local politics is one way to bring about change. Seek out every opportunity to voice your concerns, and demand that your government representatives account for their actions. Be relentless.

Get organized. You can overcome the governmental behemoth with enough cunning, skill and organization.

Play to your strengths and assets. Conduct strategy sessions with others to develop both the methods and ways to force change.

Be creative. Be bold and imaginative, for this is guerilla warfare—not to be fought with tanks and guns but through creative methods of dissent and resistance. Creatively responding to circumstances will often be one of your few resources if you are to be an effective agent of change.

Use the media. Effective use of the media is essential. Attracting media coverage not only enhances and magnifies your efforts, it is a valuable education tool. It publicizes your message to a much wider audience. It is through the media—television, newspapers, internet sites, bloggers, and so on—that people find out about your growing resistance movement.

Start brushfires for freedom. Recognize that you don't have to go it alone. Engage those around you in discussions about issues of importance. Challenge them to be part of a national dialogue. One person at a city planning meeting with a protest sign is an irritant. Three individuals at the same meeting with the same sign are a movement. You will find that those in power fear and respect numbers.

Take action. Be prepared to mobilize at a moment's notice. It doesn't matter who you are, where you're located or what resources are at your disposal. What matters is that you recognize the problems and care enough to do something about them. Whether you're 8, 28 or 88, you have something unique to contribute. You don't have to be a hero. You just have to show up and be ready to take action.

Be forward-looking. Develop a vision for the future. Is what you're hoping to achieve enduring? Have you developed a plan to continue to educate others about the problems you're hoping to tackle and ensure that others will continue in your stead?

Develop fortitude. What is it that led to the successful protest movements of the past? Resolve and the refusal to be put off. When the time came, Martin Luther King, Jr., for one, was willing to take to the streets for what he believed and even go to jail if necessary. King risked having an arrest record by committing acts of nonviolent civil disobedience. He was willing to sacrifice himself. But first, he had to develop the intestinal fortitude to give him the strength to stand and fight. If you decide that you don't have the requisite fortitude, find someone who does and back them.

Be selfless and sacrificial. Freedom is not free—there is always a price to be paid and a sacrifice to be made. If any movement is to be truly successful, it must be manned by individuals who seek a greater good and do not waver from their purposes.

Remain optimistic, and keep hope alive. Although our rights are increasingly coming under attack, we still have certain freedoms. We can still fight back. We have the right to dissent, to protest and even to vigorously criticize or oppose the government and its laws.

The key to making a difference is in understanding that the first step begins with you. As Mahatma Gandhi said, "We need to be the change we wish to see in the world."[3]

CHAPTER NINETEEN

COMPLIANT LAMBS OR NONVIOLENT GADFLIES?

"We must see the need of having nonviolent gadflies."
—Martin Luther King, Jr.[1]

When it comes to the staggering loss of civil liberties, the Constitution hasn't changed. Rather, as we have seen, it is the American people who have changed.

Once a citizenry that generally fomented a rebellion and founded a country, Americans are no longer the people they once were. Americans today live in a glass dome, says author Nicholas von Hoffman, a kind of terrarium, cut off from both reality and the outside world. In his words, they are "bobbleheads in Bubbleland. They shop in bubbled malls, they live in gated communities, and they move from place to place breathing their own private air in bubble-mobiles known as SUVs."[2]

Like lambs to the slaughter, too many Americans march in lockstep with whatever the government dictates, believing that to be patriotism. And those who do get a bit rowdy in voicing their disagreement with government policies find themselves labeled "troublemakers" and made into easy targets for attack by the media, politicians and the like.

In the past, however, it has been the so-called troublemakers—those rowdy protesters who challenge the status quo—who have actually changed things for the better in America. When Birmingham, Alabama, became the epicenter of the civil rights struggle for African-Americans, Martin Luther King, Jr. and others participated in peaceful protests such as mass marches and sit-ins. The police response was repression in the form of tear gas, dogs, fire hoses, and arrests, including that of King.

Yet as King acknowledged in his April 1963 "Letter from Birmingham Jail," demonstrations and objections to the status quo are sometimes necessary. Still, King was opposed to violent protests, preferring instead to encourage "tension." As he wrote: "there is a type of constructive, nonviolent tension which is necessary for growth … we must see the need of having nonviolent gadflies to create the kind of tension in society that will help men to rise from the dark depths of prejudice and racism to the majestic heights of understanding and brotherhood."[3]

King's philosophy was undergirded by civil disobedience. This means of nonviolent resistance was used to great effect by Mahatma Gandhi in his campaign for Indian independence from the British, in South Africa in the fight against apartheid, and of course by the civil rights movement, to name but three examples. Civil disobedience was also used to great effect at the Boston Tea Party.

Protests can take the form of stopping traffic, sit-ins, and other non-verbal forms of expression. The key, however, is standing on principle without wavering. As Henry David Thoreau wrote in his *Resistance to Civil Government, or Civil Disobedience*, inactivity by citizens can be more harmful to society than revolution:

> There are thousands who are *in opinion* opposed to slavery and to the war, who yet in effect do nothing to put an end to them; who, esteeming themselves children of Washington and Franklin, sit down with their hands in their pockets, and say that they know not what to do, and do nothing … They hesitate, and they regret, and sometimes they petition; but they do nothing in earnest and with effect. They will wait, well disposed, for others to remedy the evil, that they may no longer have it to regret.[4]

Thoreau goes on to note that for protest to be effective, it doesn't need to use force:

> If a thousand men were not to pay their tax bills this year, that would not be a bloody and violent measure, as it would be to pay them, and enable the State to commit violence and shed innocent blood. This is, in fact, the definition of a peaceable revolution.[5]

Peaceable or not, the United States has a long history of revolutionary and reactionary behavior. Thomas Jefferson was one such rebel. "What country before ever existed a century and a half without a rebellion? And what country can preserve it's liberties if their rulers are not warned from time to time that their people preserve the spirit of resistance?" Jefferson wrote. "Let them take arms.... What signify a few lives lost in a century or two? The tree of liberty must be refreshed from time to time with the blood of patriots and tyrants."[6]

The figurative message of Jefferson's words should be heeded by all. His words illustrate the importance of political action. Jefferson, like Thoreau, hated inaction and stasis. Each of these men believed that the status quo should be challenged when it was found lacking, and overturned when it yielded unjust results. Embracing that spirit today might lead to civil disobedience, but surely from time to time that is necessary. Without it, the civil rights movement would never have succeeded, the colonies of the United States would never have broken free from their British oppressor, and India might never have gained her independence.

Thomas Jefferson and those who followed took it as a rule of thumb that political progress stems from dissent. Under the First Amendment, people have a right to dissent. The great dissenters such as Martin Luther King, Jr. were even willing to commit civil disobedience to force the government to assume its constitutional role.

But as author Howard Zinn points out all too well, "Civil disobedience is not our problem. Our problem is civil obedience."[7]

NOTES

INTRODUCTION: WHAT PATRIOTS DO

1. Barbara Ehrenreich, *The Worst Years of Our Lives: Irreverent Notes from a Decade of Greed* (Pantheon Books, 1991), p. 11.
2. James Washington, ed., *A Testament of Hope: The Essential Writings and Speeches of Martin Luther King, Jr.* (HarperSanFrancisco, 1991), p. 298.
3. Earl Warren, *A Republic, If You Can Keep It* (Quadrangle Books, 1972), p. 104.
4. *United States v. Schwimmer*, 279 U.S. 644, 654-55 (1929) (Holmes, J., *dissenting*).
5. Warren, *op. cit.*, pp. 6-7.
6. G.M. Gilbert, *Nuremberg Diary* (Farrar, Straus and Co., 1947), pp. 278-9.

PART ONE

CHAPTER 1: WHAT IT MEANS TO BE AN AMERICAN

1. Henry David Thoreau, *A Yankee in Canada* (Houghton Mifflin, 1892), p. 111.
2. *See*, for example, "Obama Image Unscathed By Terrorism Controversy," *Pew Research Center for the People and the Press* (Jan. 14, 2010). Web. Aug. 25 2010. <http://pewresearch.org/pubs/1463/poll-terrorism-policies-health-care-obama-issues-personal-image>.
3. *As quoted in* Morris Berman, *Dark Ages America: The Final Phase of Empire* (W.W. Norton and Co., 2006), p. 13.
4. Letter of Thomas Jefferson to Robert C. Weightman (June 24, 1826). ME 16;182.
5. Chalmers Johnson, *Nemesis: The Last Days of the American Republic* (Metropolitan Books, 2006), pp. 13-14.

CHAPTER 2: THE STATE OF THE NATION

1. Bertram Gross, *Friendly Fascism: The New Face of Power in America* (South End Press, 1980), p. 3.
2. "Congressman: Superhighway about North American Union," *World Net Daily* (Oct. 30, 2006). Web. Aug. 25, 2010. < http://www.wnd.com/?pageId=38614>.
3. Rowenna Davis, "Making life worth living," *The Guardian* (Jan. 5. 2009). Web. Aug. 25, 2010. <http://www.guardian.co.uk/commentisfree/2009/jan/05/youngpeople-mentalhealth>.

CHAPTER 3: HOW LUCKY IT IS FOR OUR POLITICIANS THAT AMERICANS DO NOT THINK

1. *As quoted* in Kelly Nickell, ed., *Pocket Patriot: Quote from American Heroes* (Writer's Digest Books, 2005), p. 125.
2. *As quoted* in Simon Blackburn, *Being Good* (Oxford University Press, 2001), p. 2.
3. Alex Marshall, *How Cities Work* (University of Texas Press, 2000), pp. 189-90.
4. "Homer Simpson, Yes; First Amendment? 'Doh!'" *Associated Press* (March 1, 2006). Web. Sep. 1, 2008 <http://www.editorandpublisher.com/eandp/news/article_display.jsp?vnu_content_id=1002113807>.
5. "The Illiteracy Time Bomb." *Business Week* (Feb. 14, 2002). Web. Aug. 25, 2010. <http://www.businessweek.com/smallbiz/content/feb2002/sb20020214_7072.htm>.
6. *As quoted* in Cal Thomas and Bob Beckel, *Common Ground: How to Stop the Partisan War That Is Destroying America* (William Morrow, 2007), p. 174.
7. *As quoted* in Edward R. Bayley, *Joe McCarthy and the Press* (University of Wisconsin Press, 1981), p. 193.

CHAPTER 4: ARE YOU AN ENEMY OF THE STATE?

1. U.S. Department of Homeland Security, "Rightwing Extremism: Current Economic and Political Climate Fueling Resurgence

in Radicalization and Recruitment," Federation of American Scientists (Apr. 7, 2009). Web. Aug. 25, 2010. <http://www.fas.org/irp/eprint/rightwing.pdf>.

2.   Nathan P. Freier, "Known Unknowns: Unconventional 'Strategic Shocks' in Defense Strategy Development," Strategic Studies Institute/United States Army War College (November 4, 2008), p. 31. Available online at <www.strategicstudiesinstitute.army.mil/pdffiles/pub890.pdf>.

3.   Steve Watson and Paul Watson, "Army 'Strategic Shock' Report Says Troops May Be Needed To Quell U.S. Civil Unrest," Infowars.net (Dec. 16, 2008). Web. 25 Aug. 2010. <http://www.prisonplanet.com/army-strategic-shock-report-says-troops-may-be-needed-to-quell-us-civil-unrest.html>.

CHAPTER 5: BIG BROTHER WANTS TO KNOW ALL ABOUT YOU

1.   Jerome Corsi, "Your Papers Please… Census Threat: $5,000 Fines," *WorldNetDaily* (Mar. 16, 2010). Web. Aug. 26, 2010. <http://www.wnd.com/index.php?fa=PAGE.view&pageId=128409>.

2.   George Orwell, *Nineteen Eighty-Four* (Harcourt, Brace & World, 1949), pp. 136-37.

CHAPTER 6: WELCOME TO THE NEW TOTAL SECURITY STATE

1.   George Orwell, *Nineteen Eighty-Four* (Harcourt Brace, & World, 1949), p. 9.

2.   *As quoted* in Robert O'Harrow, Jr., *No Place to Hide* (Free Press, 2005), p. 9.

3.   Jeffrey Rosen, "A Cautionary Tale for a New Age of Surveillance," *New York Times* (Oct. 7, 2001). Web. Aug. 25, 2010. <http://www.nytimes.com/2001/10/07/magazine/07SURVEILLANCE.html>.

4.   James Bamford, "The New Thought Police: The NSA Wants to Know How You Think—Maybe Even What You Think," *NOVA* (Jan. 1. 2009). Web. Aug 25, 2010. <http://www.pbs.org/wgbh/nova/military/nsa-police.html>.

CHAPTER 7: SCANNERS: NO PLACE TO HIDE

1. *As quoted* in Leonard Peikoff, *The Ominous Parallels: The End of Freedom in America* (Random House, 1983), p. 47.
2. Christine Vendel, "High-tech wow for police is a privacy worry for some," *Kansas City Star* (Aug. 1, 2010). Accessed on Aug. 28, 2010, at http://webcache.googleusercontent. com/search?q=cache:gHdF8myNonAJ:www.kansascity. com/2010/08/01/2121998_high-tech-wow-for-police-is-a. html%3Fstorylink%3Domni_popular+%22High-tech+wow+for+ police+is+a+privacy+worry+for+some%22&cd=1&hl=en&ct=cl nk&gl=us.
3. Andy Greenberg, "Full-Body Scan Technology Deployed In Street-Roving Vans," *Forbes* (Aug. 24, 2010). Accessed on Sept. 8, 2010, at http://blogs.forbes.com/andygreenberg/2010/08/24/full-body-scan-technology-deployed-in-street-roving-vans/.
4. Leonora LaPeter Anton, "Airport body scanners reveal all, but what about when it's your kid?" *St. Petersburg Times* (July 18, 2010). Accessed on Sept. 8, 2010, at http://www.tampabay.com/ news/transportation/airport-body-scanners-reveal-all-but-what-about-when-its-your-kid/1109659.
5. Joe Sharkey, "Annoyances Mount Over the Body Scanner," *New York Times* (July 19, 2010). Accessed on Sept. 8, 2010, at http://www.nytimes.com/2010/07/20/business/20road.html?_ r=2&scp=1&sq=airport%20scanners&st=cse.
6. James Ridgeway, "The Great Airport Scanner Scam," *Pacific Free Press* (Jan. 5, 2010). Accessed on Sept. 8, 2010, at http://www. pacificfreepress.com/news/1/5335-the-great-airport-scanner-scam. html.
7. Clark Hoyt, "The Sources' Stake in the News," *New York Times* (Jan. 16, 2010). Accessed on Sept. 8, 2010, at http://www.nytimes. com/2010/01/17/opinion/17pubed.html?_r=1&scp=1&sq=airport+ scanner+manufacturer&st=nyt.

CHAPTER 8: THE MARK OF THE BEAST?

1. Charles E. Schumer and Lindsey O. Graham, "The right way

to mend immigration." *The Washington Post* (Mar. 19, 2010). Web. Aug. 25, 2010. < http://www.washingtonpost.com/wp-dyn/content/article/2010/03/17/AR2010031703115.html>.

2. Megan Carpenter, "The Government Would Like to See Your Papers, Please." *The Washington Independent* (Mar. 9, 2010). Web. Aug. 25, 2010. <http://washingtonindependent.com/78760/the-government-would-like-to-see-your-papers-please>.

CHAPTER 9: THE GLOBAL POLICE

1. Virginia State Constitutional Convention, December 1, 1829.
2. "Analysis Of The Obama Interpol Order," *Rense.com* (Dec. 24, 2009). Web. Aug. 25, 2010. <http://www.rense.com/general88/interpols.htm>.
3. James Madison, *Memorial and Remonstrance* (1785). Available online at <http://www.infidels.org/library/historical/james_madison/memorial.html.>.
4. Bertram Gross, *Friendly Fascism: The New Face of Power in America* (South End Press, 1980), p. 3.

CHAPTER 10: SECRET PRISONS IN AMERICA

1. John F. Kennedy, *Address Before the American Newspapers Association* (Apr. 27, 1961). Available online at <http://www.jfklibrary.org/Historical+Resources/Archives/Reference+Desk/Speeches/JFK/003POF03NewspaperPublishers04271961.htm>.
2. Bob Herbert, "Big Brother in Blue," *New York Times* (Mar. 13, 2010). Web. Aug. 25 2010. <http://www.nytimes.com/2010/03/13/opinion/13herbert.html>.
3. Jacqueline Stevens, "America's Secret ICE Castles," *The Nation* (Dec. 16, 2009). Web. Aug. 25, 2010. <http://www.thenation.com/article/americas-secret-ice-castles>.
4. *Ibid.*
5. *Ibid.*
6. Tyche Hendricks, "US Citizens Wrongly Detained, Deported by ICE," *San Francisco Chronicle* (July 27, 2009). Web. Aug. 25, 2010. < http://articles.sfgate.com/2009-07-27/news/17218849_1_judy-rabinovitz-immigration-laws-illegal-immigrant>.

7.   *Ibid.*
8.   Stevens, *op. cit.*
9.   Alexander Hamilton, *The Federalist* 84 (May 28, 1788).

CHAPTER 11: POLICE OVERKILL

1.   Mary M. Chapman and Susan Saulny, "Tragedy in Detroit, With Reality TV Crew in Tow," *New York Times* (May 21, 2010). Web. Aug. 25, 2010. <http://www.nytimes.com/2010/05/22/us/22detroit.html>.
2.   "Family: 7-year-old shot by police was asleep," Associated Press (May 17, 2010).
3.   Chapman, *op. cit.*
4.   Radley Balko, "Paramilitary police don't make us safer," *The Washington Times* (Apr. 15, 2010). Web. Aug. 25, 2010. < http://www.washingtontimes.com/news/2010/apr/15/paramilitary-police-dont-make-us-safer/>.
5.   *Ibid.*
6.   "Arkansas Police Use Taser on 10-Year-Old Girl," Associated Press (Nov. 18, 2009).
7.   Rosemary Black, "Georgia police taser Clifford Grevemberg, an autistic teen with a heart condition," *New York Daily News* (May 24, 2010). Web. Aug. 25, 2010, <http://www.nydailynews.com/news/national/2010/05/24/2010-05-24_georgia_police_taser_clifford_grevemberg_an_autistic_teen_with_a_heart_condition.html>.
8.   David Kravets, "Court OKs Repeated Tasering of Pregnant Woman," *Wired* (March 29, 2010). Web. Aug. 25, 2010. <http://www.wired.com/threatlevel/2010/03/pregnant_woman_tasered/>.
9.   *See* John W. Whitehead, *The Change Manifesto: Join the Block by Block Movement to Remake America* (Sourcebooks, 2008), pp. 47-50.

CHAPTER 12: THE GROUNDWORK HAS BEEN LAID FOR MARTIAL LAW

1.   "Farewell Address to the Nation," Jan. 17, 1961. Available online at <http://mcadams.posc.mu.edu/ike.htm >.

2.   Charlie Savage, "Obama's War on Terror May Resemble Bush's in Some Areas," *New York Times* (Feb. 17, 2009). Web. Aug. 25, 2010. <http://www.nytimes.com/2009/02/18/us/politics/18policy.html>.

3.   *See* John W. Whitehead, *The Change Manifesto: Join the Block by Block Movement to Remake America* (Sourcebooks, 2008), pp. 43-44.

4.   Johnny Johnson, "Oklahoma City police officer pulls man over for anti-Obama sign on vehicle," *The Oklahoman* (Feb. 19, 2009). Web. Aug. 25, 2010. <http://newsok.com/okc-officer-pulls-man-over-for-anti-obama-sign-on-vehicle/article/3347038 >.

5.   Gina Cavallaro, "Brigade homeland tours start Oct. 1," *Army Times* (Sept. 30, 2008). Web. Aug. 25, 2010. <http://www.armytimes.com/news/2008/09/army_homeland_090708w/>.

6.   Spencer S. Hsu, "Local Police Want Right to Jam Wireless Signals," *The Washington Post* (Feb. 1. 2009). Web. Aug. 25, 2010. <http://www.washingtonpost.com/wp-dyn/content/article/2009/01/31/AR2009013101548.html>.

7.   Chris Hedges, "Bad News From America's Top Spy," *Truthdig* (Feb. 16, 2009). Web. Aug. 25, 2010. <http://www.truthdig.com/report/item/20090216_bad_news_from_americas_top_spy/>.

PART TWO

CHAPTER 13: WILL OUR FREEDOMS SURVIVE?

1.   Cullen Murphy, *Are We Rome? The Fall of an Empire and the Fate of America* (Houghton Mifflin Harcourt, 2007), p. 12.

2.   "Millennials: A Portrait of Generation Next," Pew Research Center (February 2010).

3.   Andrew Kohut, "POLL: Millennials: Confident. Connected. Open to Change," Pew Research Center (Feb. 23, 2010).

4.   "Millennials," *op. cit.*

5.   Raina Kelley, "Generation Me," *Newsweek* (Apr. 18, 2009). Web. Aug. 25, 2010. <http://www.newsweek.com/2009/04/17/generation-me.html>.

CHAPTER 14: TEACHING TOTALITARIANISM

1.   *Ginzburg v. United States*, 383 U.S. 463, 498 (1966).
2.   "More Teens Can Name Three Stooges Than Can Name Three Branches of Government," National Constitution Center (Sept. 2, 1998).
3.   "Survey Finds First Amendment Is Being Left Behind in U.S. High Schools," John S. and James L. Knight Foundation. Available online at < http://firstamendment.jideas.org/downloads/future_final.pdf>.
4.   "First Amendment no big deal, students say," Associated Press (Jan. 31, 2005).
5.   Brandon Shulleeta, "AHS papers tossed after editorial," *Daily Progress* (June 18, 2010). Web. Aug. 25, 2010. <http://www2.dailyprogress.com/news/cdp-news-local/2010/jun/18/ahs_papers_tossed_after_editorial-ar-319356/>.
6.   Steven G. Vegh, "Two Norfolk teachers put on leave over material about police," *The Virginian-Pilot* (May 27, 2010). Web. Aug. 25, 2010 < http://hamptonroads.com/2010/05/two-norfolk-teachers-put-leave-over-material-about-police>.
7.   *The War on Kids* (Spectacle Films, 2009), www.thewaronkids.com.

CHAPTER 15: WHY AREN'T SCHOOLS TEACHING OUR CHILDREN THEIR RIGHTS AND FREEDOMS?

1.   Letter of Thomas Jefferson to Richard Price, 1789. ME 7:253
2.   "75 Percent of Oklahoma High School Students Can't Name the First President of the U.S." *Newson6.com* (Sept. 21, 2009). Web. Aug. 25, 2010. <http://www.newson6.com/Global/story.asp?S=11141949>.
3.   "Study of Civic Education in Arizona," Arizona Civics Coalition and The Center for Civic Education and Leadership. Available online at < http://ccel.asu.edu/assets/documents/AZ_Civics_Study.pdf>.
4.   "The Shaping of the American Mind," Intercollegiate Studies Institute. Available online at <http://www.americancivicliteracy.org/2010/major_findings_finding1.html>.

5. Letter of Thomas Jefferson to William Jarvis (September 28, 1820). ME 15:278.

6. Thomas Jefferson, James Madison, et al. in *Report to the Commissioners Appointed to fix the Site of the University of Virginia* (August 4, 1810). Available online at <http://press-pubs. uchicago.edu/founders/documents/v1ch18s33.html>.

7. *Ibid.*

PART THREE

CHAPTER 16: SEVEN PRINCIPLES FOR FREE GOVERNMENT

1. Letter of Thomas Jefferson to James Madison, 1787. ME: 6:392.

2. "James Madison's Notes from the Constitutional Convention" (July 11, 1787). Available online at <http://www.usd116.org/ ProfDev/AHTC/lessons/Foley08/FOLEY-convention%20 transcript.pdf>.

3. *The Writings of Thomas Jefferson.* Ed. Andrew A. Lipscomb and Albert Ellery Bergh. 20 vols. Washington: Thomas Jefferson Memorial Association, 1905. Alternatively: *Kentucky Resolution* (1798. ME 17:388)

4. "Nixon's Views on Presidential Power: Excerpts from an interview with David Frost," (May 19, 1971). Available online at <http:// www.landmarkcases.org/nixon/nixonview.html>.

5. Alexis de Tocqueville, *Democracy in America* (Harper Perennial, 1988), p. 63.

CHAPTER 17: KNOW YOUR RIGHTS OR YOU WILL LOSE THEM

1. Letter of Thomas Jefferson to William Stevens Smith, 1788. FE 5:3.

2. Nat Hentoff, "Fierce Watchdog of the Constitution," *The Village Voice* (Aug. 5, 2003). Web. Aug. 25, 2010. < http://www. villagevoice.com/2003-08-05/news/fierce-watchdog-of-the-constitution/>.

CHAPTER 18: WHAT KIND OF REVOLUTIONARY WILL YOU BE?

1. James Washington, ed., *A Testament of Hope: The Essential Writings and Speeches of Martin Luther King, Jr.* (HarperSanFrancisco, 1991), p. 292.

2. *See* John W. Whitehead, *The Change Manifesto: Join the Block by Block Movement to Remake America* (Sourcebooks, 2008), pp. 225-234.

3. Carmella B'Hahn, "Be the change you wish to see: An interview with Arun Gandhi," *Reclaiming Children and Youth* [Bloomington] Vol.10, No. 1 (Spring 2001) p. 6.

CHAPTER 19: COMPLIANT LAMBS OR NONVIOLENT GADFLIES?

1. James Washington, ed., *A Testament of Hope: The Essential Writings and Speeches of Martin Luther King, Jr.* (HarperSanFrancisco, 1991), p. 291.

2. As quoted in Morris Berman, *Dark Ages America: The Final Phase of Empire* (W.W. Norton and Co., 2006), p. 282.

3. Washington, *op. cit.*

4. Henry David Thoreau, "Resistance to Civil Government." (1849). Reprinted in *Walden, Civil Disobedience, and Other Writings*. Ed. William Rossi. (W.W. Norton 2008) p. 231

5. *Ibid.*

6. Letter of Thomas Jefferson to William Stephens Smith, 1787. ME 6:373.

7. Howard Zinn, *Failure to Quit.* (South End Press, 2002), p. 45.

ABOUT THE AUTHOR

Constitutional attorney and author John W. Whitehead is widely recognized as one of the nation's most vocal and involved civil liberties attorneys. Whitehead's approach to civil liberties issues has earned him numerous accolades and accomplishments, including the Hungarian Medal of Freedom and the 2010 Milner S. Ball Lifetime Achievement Award for "[his] decades of difficult and important work, as well as [his] impeccable integrity in defending civil liberties for all." Whitehead's concern for the persecuted and oppressed led him, in 1982, to establish The Rutherford Institute, a nonprofit civil liberties and human rights organization whose international headquarters are located in Charlottesville, Virginia.

Whitehead has also written, debated and practiced widely in the area of constitutional law, human rights and popular culture. Whitehead's weekly commentaries, carried by daily and weekly newspapers and web publications across the country, take the pulse of the nation, of what's happening and what's news. Audio versions of Whitehead's commentaries are also made available to radio stations across the country. And his weekly video blogs, distributed through YouTube, are gaining in viewership and popularity.

Whitehead is the author of some 20 books, including *The Change Manifesto* (Sourcebooks, 2008). Whitehead's articles examining trends and issues have been printed in such newspapers as the *Los Angeles Times, New York Times, Washington Post, Washington Times* and *USA Today*. Whitehead has been a frequent commentator on a variety of legal and cultural issues in the national media. He has been interviewed by the national and international media, including *CNN Headline News, Larry King Live, 60 Minutes,* and *National Public Radio*.